T0162677

TRUTH &
CONSEQUENCES

TRUTH &
CONSEQUENCES

RALPH E. CARLSON

TRUTH AND CONSEQUENCES

Scripture quotations marked NIV are taken from the Holy Bible, New International Version®. NIV®. Copyright © 1973, 1978, 1984 by International Bible Society. Used by permission of Zondervan. All rights reserved. [Biblica]

iUniverse books may be ordered through booksellers or by contacting:

iUniverse
1663 Liberty Drive
Bloomington, IN 47403
www.iuniverse.com
1-800-Authors (1-800-288-4677)

Because of the dynamic nature of the Internet, any web addresses or links contained in this book may have changed since publication and may no longer be valid. The views expressed in this work are solely those of the author and do not necessarily reflect the views of the publisher, and the publisher hereby disclaims any responsibility for them.

Any people depicted in stock imagery provided by Thinkstock are models, and such images are being used for illustrative purposes only. Certain stock imagery © Thinkstock.

ISBN: 978-1-4917-7318-5 (sc)
ISBN: 978-1-4917-7319-2 (e)

Library of Congress Control Number: 2015911963

Print information available on the last page.

iUniverse rev. date: 08/07/2015

TO

Kay, Jeff, Brad, Julie, Jen, Debra, Ryne, Brant, Jordan, and Abby.

Special Thanks

Dr. Jim Platt. Pastor Jay Passavant, Pastor Scott Stevens, Pastor Kent Chevalier, Dr. David Jones, Dr. Gary Smith, Dr. Jan Dudt, Stephanie, Thomas, and Peter.

Contents

1

Introduction

Have you ever asked yourself the question, does God exist? Have you ever wondered about the source of life on earth, and in particular, human life?

These questions were the subject of a conference sponsored by the Center for Vision and Values at Grove City College. Three basic approaches which attempt to answer these questions were discussed.

+ Creationism
+ Intelligent design
+ Evolution

After attending this conference I felt challenged to dig deeper into these approaches and to analyze the voracity of their arguments. Evolutionists claim that all complex life has evolved from simple life forms over billions of years. They are adamant that their claim has been proven to be a scientific fact.

As a Professor of Mathematics I have spent considerable time working with students to help them develop logically correct arguments in constructing proofs. A careful analysis of the arguments posed by evolutionists revealed that they have a logical error in their 'proof' that evolution is a scientific fact. This logical error is described in detail in chapter 2. A simple example from Major League Baseball is provided to illustrate the fallacy in their argument.

In addition to the fallacy in their so-called proof, there are two other deficiencies in their argument that are well known. First, evolutionists have no explanation concerning how living organisms came into existence from nonliving materials. Second, the fossil record does not support the existence of the many transitional species that would be necessary for the progression from simple life forms to the complex life forms present in the world today. Evolutionists admit both of these deficiencies. However, despite these shortcomings and the logical error in their proof, this does not mean that evolution is false. It simply means that at this point in time, their claim is merely a conjecture and not a scientific fact. Creationism and intelligent design also should be classified as conjectures.

Instead of attempting to answer the question concerning the existence of God, there is another approach which involves transforming the question into a proposition. A proposition is a statement that is either true or false. There is no middle ground. Thus, a proposition has a truth value: it is true or false. Period. Then the consequences of the two possible truth values can be analyzed.

There is a wide variety of interpretations and understandings of the word 'God'. In order to compensate for this ambiguity the first question is transformed into the following proposition:

Proposition 1: An infinite, intelligent entity (IIE) exists.

What a person believes to be the truth value of Proposition 1 has no impact on its actual truth value. However, the truth value together with what a person believes about the truth value can have a profound impact on that person's life, and quite possibly on what happens to that person after he or she dies.

If Proposition 1 is false, then all religions that worship a Supernatural Being—including Christianity, Judaism, and Islam—are false. Evolutionists are probably correct in their belief that living organisms came into existence from nonliving materials, and that all complex life has evolved from simpler life forms over billions of years. If Proposition 1 is false, there was no Creator. There was no Intelligent Designer. Humans are merely an accident of nature. Every person will suffer the same fate so this ultimately leads to a dead end for all humans because there is no such thing as life after death.

If Proposition 1 is true, then the second question can be transformed into the following proposition:

Proposition 2: The IIE created life on earth, including human life.

If Proposition 2 is false, then the IIE played no role in the creation of life on earth, and the consequences are similar to those if Proposition 1 is false. Thus, if Proposition 2 is false, this too leads to a dead end.

However, if there is an IIE who created life on earth—and in particular, human life—then there was some underlying purpose for this conscious act. One possible purpose leads to Proposition 3.

Proposition 3: There is life after death.

If Propositions 1 and 2 are true but Proposition 3 is false, then this result also leads to a dead end for humankind. If there is no life after death, why did the IIE create life, and in particular human life, in the first place?

However, if all three propositions are true, then what does life after death entail? One possible form for life after death is reincarnation which is the belief that after physical death the soul or the spirit takes on new life in a different body. Buddhists and Hindus believe in reincarnation.

Christians, Jews, and Muslims believe there are two possibilities for life after death: heaven and hell. In heaven one spends eternity in the magnificent presence of the Creator in an existence far beyond our wildest dreams. In hell one spends eternity apart from the Creator in an existence far beyond our worst nightmare.

Where a person spends eternity is determined by what that person believes and how that person lives. For Christians the answer is articulated in John 3:16 and John 14:6. (All biblical references are from the NIV Study Bible.)

> For God so loved the world that he gave his only Son, that whoever believes in Him shall not perish but have everlasting life. (John 3:16)

> Jesus answered, 'I am the way, the truth, and the life. No
> one comes to the Father except through me. (John 14:6).

How one's fate is determined as found in the Bible leads to a fourth proposition.

Proposition 4: Jesus, the Son of God as described in the New Testament, was a living being who came to earth approximately 2,000 years ago.

If Proposition 4 is false, then Christianity is not a valid religion. If Proposition 4 is true, then Christianity is true and the IIE is referred to as God.

Creationism, Intelligent Design, and Evolution are described in more detail in chapter 2. The four propositions and some of the consequences of their respective truth values are discussed in chapters 3 and 4.

If all four propositions are true, then there should be strong evidence that God exists and is active in the world today. Direct and indirect evidence supporting this conclusion is presented in chapter 5. Although the evidence does not rise to the level of scientific proof that God exists, this evidence cannot be denied.

The United States has a very strong Judeo-Christian heritage. The vast majority of our founding fathers believed that all four of these propositions were true. European authors such as Alexis de Tocqueville, Achille Murat, and Harriet Martineau were amazed at how deep Christianity was embedded in American culture and governance.

However, a careful examination of American culture and society today clearly reveals that Christianity is under unprecedented attack. These attacks are based on a distorted perception of the Establishment Clause in the First Amendment to the Constitution and in the concept of separation of church and state. The proponents of these attacks often use tactics that are championed by Saul Alinsky in his book, *Rules for Radicals* (1971).

One of the reasons why our society has changed and the attackers have enjoyed considerable success is because many people are either ignorant of our Judeo-Christian foundation or they have chosen to ignore it.

Rabbi Jonathan Cahn observed that in many ways America has been following the same path that ancient Israel followed thousands of years ago. The Israelites ignored their religious heritage and adopted many of the customs and beliefs that went against the laws handed down by Moses. Elijah, Elisha, Hosea, and Amos were prophets who challenged the Israelites to repent or face the loss of God's blessing and shield of protection. The Israelites chose to ignore those warnings. Israel was invaded by Assyria in 732BC and suffered devastating losses. Then Assyria withdrew most of its forces and Israel gained a brief respite The prophet Isaiah proclaimed that the attack was a warning by God, and the Israelites needed to repent or Israel would face future destruction. However, the Israelites did not repent. Instead, they rebuilt their cities in an attempt to become stronger so they could repel future attacks. Their efforts were in vain. A decade later Assyria attacked once again. This time Assyria conquered Israel, and many Israelites were exiled to neighboring countries in the Middle East.

In his book, *The Harbinger: The Ancient Mystery that holds the Secret of America's Future* (2011) and the associated video, *Isaiah 9:10*, Rabbi Jonathan Cahn cites nine harbingers that God gave Israel involving the initial invasion by Assyria. Cahn then compared these warnings by God to the terrorist attack on America on September 11, 2001. The stunning parallels between Assyria's attack on Israel and the warnings God gave to ancient Israel and aspects of the attacks on America on 9/11 led Rabbi Cahn to conclude that the attack on 9/11 was a warning by God that America must repent or face the same fate as ancient Israel. Rabbi Cahn's conjecture leads to Proposition 5.

Proposition 5: The terrorist attack of 9/11 was a warning by God for America to repent and return to its Judeo-Christian heritage or face future destruction.

If this proposition is true, and if America does not repent, then the potential consequences are truly frightening.

The bottom line is that each of us must address the truth value of Proposition 1. If Proposition 1 is false, everyone faces the same fate. If Proposition 1 is true and if either Proposition 2 or 3 is false, the results are similar. However, if the first three propositions are true, then life takes on a dramatic new meaning and a person's response to Proposition 4 will have a dramatic impact, not only on his or her life on earth but through all eternity. If Proposition 5 is also true, then this will have a dramatic effect on the future of America.

2

Creationism, Intelligent Design, and Evolution

In Chapter 1 the following questions were raised. Does God exist? What is the origin of life on earth, and in particular, human life? These questions are closely connected because an answer to one question often serves as the basis for an answer to the other question. For many people the answers to these questions are supplied by their religious beliefs. Nevertheless, it is human nature to attempt to validate religious beliefs through scientific research. Similarly, those who do not believe in God have searched for scientific proof to validate their belief that God does not exist and that life on earth is not the result of any action by a supernatural being.

Three approaches that attempt to answer these questions are creationism, intelligent design, and evolution which are described below.

Creationism: Creationists assert that God exists. Hence, they answer the first question in the affirmative. Because Creationists also believe that the Bible is the Word of God, the answer to the second question is contained in the first three chapters of the book of Genesis.

> In the beginning God created the heavens and the earth. Now the earth was formless and empty, darkness was over the surface of the deep, and the Spirit of God was hovering over the waters. (Genesis 1:1–2).

> So God created the great creatures of the sea and every living and moving thing with which the water teems, according to their kinds, and every winged bird according to its kind. (Genesis 1:21)

> God made the wild animals according to their kinds, the
> livestock, according to their kinds, and all the creatures
> that move along the ground according to their kinds.
> (Genesis 1:25)

> So God created man in his own image, in the image of
> God he created him; male and female he created them.
> (Genesis 1:27).

The first chapter of Genesis describes creation as occurring in stages over a six-day period. The culmination of the creation event was the creation of male and female in the image of God.

Creationists can be divided into two groups: Young Earth and Old Earth. Young Earth Creationists believe that God created heaven and earth in six twenty-four hour days. They believe that this creation event occurred approximately 6,000 years ago based upon the genealogy found in the book of Genesis. Old Earth Creationists believe that the earth is about 4 billion years old, and that God's creation event took place over millions of years. They believe that the days in the first chapter of Genesis are actually substantially longer periods of time, not twenty-four hours in length.

Intelligent Design: Proponents of Intelligent Design believe that scientific research has shown that even single-celled species possess an irreducible level of complexity, and that certain features of more complex life forms also are irreducibly complex. Michael Behe, one of the leading proponents of Intelligent Design, explains the concept of irreducible complexity as follows:

> By *irreducibly complex* I mean a single system composed
> of several well-matched, interacting parts that contribute
> to the basic function, wherein the removal of any one
> of the parts causes the system to effectively cease
> functioning. An irreducibly complex system cannot be
> produced directly (that is, by continuously improving
> the initial function, which continues to work by the
> same mechanism) by slight, successive modifications of a

precursor system, because any precursor to an irreducibly complex system that is missing a part is by definition nonfunctional.[1]

Because even single-celled creatures are irreducibly complex, the probability that living organisms evolved from inanimate objects, or that certain features of more complex life forms evolved from more primitive species is infinitesimally small. Hence, the only plausible explanation is that an Intelligent Designer created the single-celled species and produced more complex life forms. Proponents of Intelligent Design claim not to hold any specific religious belief, but they insist that scientific evidence supports their conclusion that an Intelligent Designer must exist. Thus, proponents of Intelligent Design answer the second question first, which they claim proves the existence of an Intelligent Designer, i.e. God.

Evolution: Evolutionists contend that life on earth has developed from simpler life-forms over billions of years, and that this statement has been proven to be a scientific fact.

Evolutionists also can be divided into two groups: Guided and Unguided. Guided Evolutionists (also called Theistic Evolutionists) believe that God exists; therefore they answer the first question in the affirmative. They also believe in the evolutionary process, although they contend that God provided some measure of direction. Hence, the evolutionary process is not totally random. In contrast, Unguided Evolutionists (also called Darwinists, Naturalists, or Atheist Evolutionists) believe that the evolutionary process can be explained by natural selection (survival of the fittest) and mutation (modified descent). Their case is based upon the proven assertion that species with a common ancestry share certain common characteristics such as molecular genetics despite differences attributable to natural selection and mutation. They argue that because all species share common characteristics, this proves that all species have a common ancestry. Also, they argue that because no supernatural being is necessary for the evolutionary process to occur, there is no evidence that God exists.

---

[1] Michael Behe, *Darwin's Black Box*, (New York: The Free Press, 1996), 39.

Thus, Creationists, proponents of Intelligent Design, and Guided Evolutionists all believe that God exists. Their primary differences involve the role that God played in the process or processes that have led to the abundance of life on earth as we know it today. Unguided Evolutionists do not believe that God exists.

Attempts to answer the two questions posed above in a scientifically rigorous manner have been tainted by injecting either religious or atheistic beliefs into what is claimed to be scientific proof'. As a result, there are strong disagreements and even vicious attacks on those who hold differing viewpoints.

> Why have we agreed so easily to call this exploded old nontheory by its cunningly chosen new disguise of "intelligent design"? There is nothing at all "intelligent" about it. It is the same old mumbo-jumbo (or in this instance, jumbo-mumbo).[2]

> This, in a nutshell, is the creationist's favourite argument – an argument that could be made only by somebody who doesn't understand the first thing about natural selection: somebody who thinks natural selection is a theory of chance whereas – in the relevant sense of chance – it is the opposite.

> The creationist misappropriation of the argument from improbability always takes the same general form, and it doesn't make any difference if the creationist chooses to masquerade in the politically expedient fancy dress of 'intelligent design' (ID).[3]

> By contrast, creationism, or "intelligent design" (its only cleverness being found in this underhanded rebranding of itself) is *not even a theory*. In all its well-financed

---

[2] Christopher Hitchens, *god is not Great*, (New York: Hatchette Book Group, 2007), 87.
[3] Richard Dawkins, *The God Delusion* (New York: First Mariner Book Edition, 2006), 138.

propaganda, it has never even attempted to show how one single piece of the natural world is explained better by "design" than by evolutionary competition. Instead, it dissolved into puerile tautology.[4]

Despite claims to the contrary by Unguided Evolutionists, to date there is no widespread agreement that any of these three approaches has been proven in a rigorous scientific manner. What follows is a brief discussion of some of the shortcomings of each approach as it is subjected to a rigorous scientific analysis.

Creationists make three assumptions which have not been proven scientifically and which may be impossible to prove scientifically:

+ God exists
+ The Bible provides an accurate portrayal of God
+ The book of Genesis provides an accurate description of creation

One additional conflict with science faced by Young Earth Creationists is their assertion that the earth is only about 6,000 years old. Most scientists believe that the earth is more than 4 billion years old based upon radioisotope and other technologies used as dating techniques. However, in his book, *Thousands ... not Billions*, Don DeYoung disputes the accuracy of commonly accepted radioisotope dating techniques. DeYoung cites the research of a group of Creationist scientists called RATE (**R**adioisotopes and the **A**ge of **T**he **E**arth) to refute conventional science.

> Over an eight-year period, the RATE team explored many aspects of radioisotope dating and the age of the earth. One fundamental conclusion is that radioactive half-lives have not remained constant throughout the earth's history. In particular, RATE research indicates nuclear decay was temporarily accelerated or speeded up on more than one occasion in the past. These suggested

---

[4] Hitchens, *god is not Great*, 86.

occasions are early during the creation week and also during the year of the Genesis flood.[5]

If nuclear decay was accelerated as DeYoung asserts, then the age of the earth would be considerably younger than the radioactive half-lives would indicate.

Contrary to the claims of Unguided Evolutionists, Intelligent Design is not creationism under another name. Intelligent Design raises an important scientific question that conflicts with the claims of Evolutionists.

> Intelligent design is three things: a scientific research program that investigates the effects of intelligent causes; an intellectual movement that challenges Darwinism and its naturalistic legacy; and a way of understanding divine action. Intelligent design therefore intersects science and theology...Many scientists think intelligent design makes for bad science (that it's just creationism in disguise) whereas many theologians think it makes for bad theology (that it misunderstands divine action). This book argues that these perceptions are mistaken and that intelligent design is just what the doctor ordered for both science and theology.[6]

However, many Unguided Evolutionists assert that ID is not science. Instead, ID simply fills in the gaps in science by assuming that these gaps were bridged by an intelligent designer.

> It is therefore unfortunate, to say the least, that the main strategy of creation propagandists is the negative one of

---

[5] Don DeYoung, *Thousands ... not Billions* (Green Forest: Master Books, Inc., 2005), 142.

[6] William Dembski, *Intelligent Design* (Downers Grove, IL: InterVarsity Press, 1999), 13.

seeking out gaps in scientific knowledge and claiming to fill them with 'intelligent design' by default.[7]

The problem with ID is that it is nothing more than a program of political and religious advocacy masquerading as science. Since a belief in the biblical God finds no support in our growing scientific understanding of the world, ID theorists invariably stake their claim on the areas of scientific ignorance.[8]

It is precisely the fact that ID has no evidence of its own, but thrives like a weed in gaps left by scientific knowledge, that sits uneasily with science's need to identify and proclaim the very same gaps as a prelude to researching them.[9]

While Intelligent Design provides some compelling evidence for the existence of an Intelligent Designer, it is virtually impossible to prove scientifically that an intelligent designer exists based solely on the argument of irreducible complexity.

Unlike Creationists and those who believe in ID, Unguided Evolutionists claim that simple life forms occurred naturally. That is, simple life forms were produced from nonliving materials through some natural process with no help from a Creator. Over a long period of time, probably billions of years, more complex life forms evolved from this common ancestry. Prominent Unguided Evolutionists such as Richard Dawkins, Sam Harris, Christopher Hitchens, and Daniel Dennett are the most dogmatic in claiming that their approach has been established beyond any reasonable doubt. They claim that evolution is not a theory, but a proven scientific fact. They claim that anyone who doubts the fact of evolution is ignoring a huge amount of scientific evidence. Consider the claims by Dennett, Harris, and Jerry Coyne.

---

[7] Dawkins, *The God Delusion*, 152.
[8] Sam Harris, *Letter to a Christian Nation* (New York: Knopf, 2007), 71-72.
[9] Dawkins, *The God Delusion*, 153.

From what sort of seed could the Tree of Life get started? That all life on earth has been produced by such a branching process of generation is now established beyond any reasonable doubt. It is as secure an example of a *scientific fact* (emphasis added) as the roundness of the Earth, thanks in large part to Darwin.[10]

We know that all complex organisms on earth, including ourselves, evolved from earlier organisms over the course of billions of years. The evidence for this is utterly overwhelming.[11]

What's *not* a problem is the lack of evidence. Since you've read this far, I hope you're convinced that evolution is far more than a scientific theory: *it is a scientific fact* (emphasis added).[12]

Dennett asserts that those who believe in God are mentally challenged and that their arguments for the existence of God are grounded on a baseless faith in a nonexistent deity.

The kindly God who lovingly fashioned each and every one of us (all creatures great and small) and sprinkled the sky with shining stars for our delight—*that* God is, like Santa Claus, a myth of childhood, not anything a sane, undeluded adult could literally believe in. *That* God must either be turned into a symbol for something less concrete or abandoned altogether.[13]

However, the alleged proof that Unguided Evolution is a scientific fact falls far short of a rigorous scientific proof for at least three reasons.

---

[10] Daniel Dennett, *Darwin's Dangerous Idea* (New York: Simon & Schuster Paperbacks, 2005), 149.

[11] Harris, *Letter to a Christian Nation*, 70.

[12] Jerry A. Coyne, *Why Evolution is True* (New York: Viking, 2009), 222.

[13] Dennett, *Darwin's Dangerous Idea*, 18.

First: Unguided Evolutionists attempt to explain how complex life forms evolved from earlier, simpler organisms over billions of years. Since simple life forms are needed to start the process, how these simple life forms came into existence is a necessary part of their argument. Unguided Evolutionists claim that these life forms came into existence from nonliving materials with no help from a Creator. To date, even under tightly controlled environments, science has not been able to create living organisms from nonliving materials. Hugh Ross makes the case as follows:

> A major flaw in the attack by radical Darwinists on the Watchmaker argument is their failure to address the origin of life. The Darwinist mechanisms of natural selection and mutations are useless *until the first life form is assembled*. In spite of decades of intense research, origin-of-life scientists have yet to demonstrate the feasibility of any mechanism(s) for the assembly of a living organism from inorganic materials by strictly natural processes.[14]

Sam Harris readily admits that Unguided Evolutionists have no explanation for the origin of life on earth.

> How the process of evolution got started is still a mystery, but that does not in the least suggest that a deity is likely to be lurking at the bottom of it all.[15]

Harris is correct that the inability to explain how life began does not prove that a supernatural being was required to begin the evolutionary process. However, this deficiency is a significant shortcoming in their 'proof' that Unguided Evolution is a scientific fact. It is quite possible that the origin of life on earth will never be answered scientifically.

Second: Because the evolutionary process is gradual, requiring billions of years, many intermediate stages or species had to be part of the transition

---

[14] Hugh Ross, *The Creator and the Cosmos* (Colorado Springs: Navpress, 1993), 102.
[15] Harris, *Letter to a Christian Nation*, 71.

from simple to more complex life forms. However, the fossil record does not support the existence of these intermediate life forms.

> The common ancestors and transitional links are still only theoretical entities, conspicuously absent from the fossil record even after long and determined searching.[16]

> The common ancestor is merely hypothetical, as are the numerous transitional intermediate forms that would have to connect such enormously different groups to the ancestor. From a Darwinist viewpoint all those hypothetical creatures are a logical necessity, but there is no empirical confirmation that they existed.[17]

> I regard the failure to find a clear "vector of progress" in life's history as the most puzzling fact of the fossil record.[18]

> "Gould and the American Museum people are hard to contradict when they say there are no transitional fossils. As a paleontologist myself, I am much occupied with the philosophical problems of identifying ancestral forms in the fossil record…I will lay it on the line—there is not one such fossil for which one could make a watertight argument".[19]

There are three possible reasons for the deficiency in the fossil record.

1. The transitional life forms did not exist
2. The transitional life forms existed, but their fossils have been destroyed.
3. The transitional life forms existed, but their fossils have not yet been discovered.

---

[16] Phillip E. Johnson, *Darwin on Trial* (Downers Grove, IL: InterVarsity Press, 1993), 100.
[17] Johnson, *Darwin on Trial*, 95.
[18] Stephen Jay Gould, quoted in *Refuting Evolution*, by Jonathan Sarfati, p. 48-49
[19] James Perloff, *The Case Against Darwin*, p. 40

Another inconsistency or anomaly in the fossil record involves the Cambrian explosion. The Cambrian explosion refers to a comparatively short period in the geologic time scale that began about 570 million years ago and ended 20 to 40 million years later. During this period a very large number of multi-celled organisms made their debut including many animal groups which we can recognize today. Jonathan Wells provides the following analysis of the Cambrian explosion relative to Unguided Evolution.

> The Cambrian explosion presents a serious challenge to Darwinian evolution. The event was remarkable because it was so abrupt and extensive—that is, because it happened so quickly, geologically speaking, and because so many major groups of animals made their debut in it. But its challenge to Darwin's theory lies not so much in its abruptness (it doesn't really matter whether it lasted 5 million years or 15 million years), or in its extent (it doesn't really matter that sponges preceded it, or that some types of worms appeared later), as in the fact that phyla and classes appeared right at the start.
>
> Darwin's theory claims that phylum – and class-level differences emerge only after a long history of divergence from lower categories such as species, genera, families, and orders. Yet the Cambrian explosion is inconsistent with this picture.[20]

A complete fossil record showing the transitions from one species to another would provide powerful evidence in an attempt to prove that Unguided Evolution is a scientific fact. Although nothing in the fossil record substantiates these transitions, Richard Dawkins, in typical fashion for Unguided Evolutionists, denies that these deficiencies are important.

> We could easily have had no fossils at all, and still the evidence for evolution from other sources, such as

---

[20] Jonathan Wells, *Icons of Evolution*, (Washington: Regnery Publishing, 2002), 41.

molecular genetics and geographical distribution, would be overwhelmingly strong.[21]

Despite Dawkins' claim the inadequacies and anomalies cited above are a second major deficiency in the "proof" that evolution is a scientific fact.

Third: Evolutionists use an invalid logical argument in their attempt to prove that all life on earth has evolved from a common ancestor. Logically correct argument forms are called rules of inference which involve propositions.

Definition 1: A *proposition* is a statement that is either true or false, but not both.[22]

The Evolutionist argument involves two propositions:

Proposition 1: Two species have a common ancestry.

Proposition 2: Two particular species have common characteristics such as molecular genetics.

The Evolutionists so-called proof consists of the following two steps.

Step 1: Prove that if Proposition 1 is true, then Proposition 2 is true. That is, prove that if two species have a common ancestry, then those species have common characteristics such as molecular genetics. Science has proven that this statement is true.

Step 2: Prove that Proposition 2 is true. That is, prove that two particular species have common characteristics such as molecular genetics.

Conclusion: Proposition 1 is true. That is, conclude that if two species have common characteristics such as molecular genetics, then those species have a common ancestry.

---

[21] Dawkins, *The God Delusion*, 154.

[22] Kenneth Rosen, *Discrete Mathematic and Its Applications*, Vol. 4 (Boston, MA: McGraw-Hill, 1999), 2.

This argument form does not produce a logically correct argument that Proposition 1 is true. It is a fallacy called affirming the conclusion. This fallacy can be illustrated using the following propositions.

Proposition 3: The Philadelphia Phillies beat the Chicago Cubs.

Proposition 4: The Phillies scored at least one run in the game against the Cubs.

Step 1: Prove that if Proposition 3 is true, then Proposition 4 is true. That is, prove that if the Phillies beat the Cubs, then the Phillies scored at least one run. This statement is true by the rules of major league baseball.

Step 2: Prove that Proposition 4 is true. That is, prove that the Phillies scored at least one run in a game against the Cubs.

Conclusion: Proposition 3 is true. That is, if the Phillies scored at least one run, then conclude that the Phillies beat the Cubs.

Scoring at least one run in a baseball game is a *necessary* condition for a team to win the game, but it is not a *sufficient* condition to guarantee victory. Even scoring 23 runs is not enough to guarantee victory because on August 25, 1922 the Phillies scored 23 runs but lost to the Cubs 26 to 23.

Similarly, two species having common characteristics such as molecular genetics is a *necessary* condition for those species to have a common ancestry, but it is not a *sufficient* condition to guarantee that those two species have a common ancestry. Even if two species have many common characteristics, this still would not prove that those species have a common ancestry. Thus, Dennett's claim that "all life on earth has been produced by a branching process is a scientific fact" is incorrect.

A much stronger statement can be made:

Just because two particular species share common characteristics such as molecular genetics, this fact alone CANNOT produce a valid, logically correct proof that those two species have a common ancestor.

19

Consider statements by Phillip Johnson and Jonathan Sarfati.

> Because Darwinists take for granted that "relationship" is equivalent to common ancestry, they assume that the molecular classifications confirm the "fact of evolution" by confirming the existence of something which by definition is caused by evolution.[23]

> We would need to find evidence that the common ancestors and transitional intermediates really existed in the living world of the past, and that natural selection in combination with random genetic changes really has the kind of creative power claimed for it. It will not be enough to find that organisms share a common biochemical basis, or that their molecules as well as their visible features can be classified in a pattern of groups within groups.[24]

> Evolution [is] a theory universally accepted not because it can be proven by logically coherent evidence to be true, but because the only alternative, special creation, is clearly incredible.[25]

> *Teaching about Evolution* avoids discussing the vast gulf between non-living matter and the first living cell, single-celled and multicelled creatures, and invertebrates and vertebrates. The gaps between these groups should be enough to show that the molecules-to-man evolution is without foundation.[26]

Sam Harris criticizes theists for not using valid, logically correct arguments to support their conclusions.

> The core of science is not controlled experiment or mathematical modeling; *it is intellectual honesty. It is time*

---

[23] Johnson, *Darwin on Trial*, 93.
[24] Johnson, *Darwin on Trial*, 91.
[25] Prof. D. M. S. Watson, quoted in, Jonathan Sarfati, *Refuting Evolution*, p. 16
[26] Jonathan Sarfati, *Refuting Evolution*, 49.

> *we acknowledged a basic feature of human discourse: when considering the truth of a proposition, one is either engaged in an honest appraisal of the evidence and logical arguments, or one isn't* (emphasis added). Religion is the one area of our lives where people imagine that some other standard of intellectual integrity applies.[27]

In reality, as the above argument demonstrates, Unguided Evolutionists also imagine that some other standard of intellectual integrity applies in their attempt to prove that evolution is a fact. Harris also claims that religion is preventing an unbiased examination of the facts.

> One of the greatest challenges facing civilization in the twenty-first century is for human beings to learn to speak about their deepest personal concerns—about ethics, spiritual experience, and the inevitability of human suffering—in ways that are not flagrantly irrational. We desperately need a public discourse that encourages critical thinking and intellectual honesty. Nothing stands in the way of this project more than the respect we accord religious faith.[28]

At the same time, Atheist Evolutionists attempt to avoid public debate by silencing the opposition in order to prevent opposing views from being made available to the general public. Consider John Patterson's comments about Creationism:

> As a matter-of-fact, creationism should be discriminated against...No advocate of such propaganda should be trusted to teach science classes or administer science programs anywhere or under any circumstances.[29]

Other examples of attempts by Unguided Evolutionists to silence their opponents are provided in chapter 4.

---

[27] Harris, *Letter to a Christian Nation*, 64-65.
[28] Harris, *Letter to a Christian Nation*, 87.
[29] John Patterson, *Journal of the National Center for Science Education*, Fall, 1983, p.19

A statement from the novel, *The Bourne Sanction*, by Eric Van Lustbader captures the actions of Unguided Evolutionists. "They have an infinite capacity for rationalizing reality to fit their personal ideas."

If Unguided Evolution is not a proven scientific fact, then how can it be characterized as an explanation for life on earth as we know it today? Consider the following definition taken from *The American College Dictionary*:

Conjecture: The formation or expression of an opinion without sufficient evidence or proof.

Because Unguided Evolutionists do not provide a valid, logically correct proof that their claim is a scientific fact, a far more accurate assessment is that, at this point in time, Unguided Evolution is merely a *conjecture*. The claims of Creationists, Intelligent Designers, and Guided Evolutionists should also be classified as conjectures.

Unguided Evolutionists such as Dawkins, Harris, Dennett, Hitchens, and others also claim that the *fact* of evolution denies the existence of a supernatural being. However, proving that something does not exist often is far more difficult than proving that something does exist.

Consider the example of extraterrestrial life forms. One way to conclusively prove that extraterrestrial life forms exist is for an alien space craft to land in some public place. Visual evidence would be in the form of TV and cellphone images, eyewitnesses, and possibly other forms of validation. Add to this list possible interviews of alien beings by members of the news media, and you would have incontrovertible proof of their existence.

Some individuals claim that the earth was visited by extraterrestrial beings near Roswell, New Mexico in July, 1947. However, no incontrovertible evidence has been brought forward, either because the government has covered it up or because such evidence never existed.

In a similar vein the SETI program has not produced any publicly available credible evidence of the existence of extraterrestrial life forms. However, the lack of credible evidence does not prove that intelligent life does not exist elsewhere in the universe just because we haven't found them—or they haven't found us.

In *God, The Failed Hypothesis*, Victor J. Stenger contends that science has proven that God does not exist. The jacket cover of his book states:

> Physicist Victor J. Stenger points out that if scientific arguments *for* the existence of God are included in the intellectual, not to mention political discourse, then arguments *against* his existence should also be considered. In *God, the Failed Hypothesis*, Stenger argues that science has advanced sufficiently to make a definitive statement on the existence—or nonexistence—of the traditional Judeo-Christian-Islamic God. He invites readers to put their minds and the scientific method to work to test this claim.
>
> By using five principal conditions for evaluating extraordinary claims, Stenger treats the existence of God like any other scientific hypothesis, stipulating that God should be detectable by scientific means, given that he is supposed to play a central role in the operation of the universe and in the lives of humans.

Stenger's attempt to prove that God does not exist is based upon the following five principal conditions:

1. Hypothesize that God plays an important role in the universe.
2. Assume that God has specific attributes that should provide objective evidence for his existence.
3. Look for such evidence with an open mind.
4. If such evidence is found, conclude that God *may* exist.
5. If such objective evidence is not found, conclude beyond a reasonable doubt that a God with these properties does *not* exist. [30]

---

[30] Victor J. Stenger, *God, The Failed Hypothesis* (Amherst, NY: Prometheus Books, 2007), 43.

Stenger's basic argument is that if God exists there should be some concrete example in which a well-established law of science has been contradicted. If such an occurrence is found, then this would be sufficient to conclude that God *may* exist (item 4 above). Because no such evidence has ever been discovered, Stenger maintains that God does not exist.

Stenger's approach raises an interesting question. What constitutes objective evidence? Does an undeniable event which has no scientific explanation qualify as objective evidence? A second question is: what constitutes a contradiction to a well-established law of science? Suppose science has no explanation for a phenomenon and cannot reproduce that phenomenon. Does this qualify as evidence that some well-established law of science has been, or at least may have been, contradicted? A key aspect of Stenger's argument is his acceptance of Unguided Evolution as a well-established fact. Stenger writes:

> Evolution by natural selection is accepted as an observed fact by the great majority of biologists and scientists in related fields, and is utilized in every aspect of modern life science including medicine. In terms of the same strict standards of empirical evidence that apply in all natural sciences, Darwinian evolution is a well-established theory that has passed many critical tests.[31]

Stenger also admits that there is no scientific explanation for the origin of life on earth.

> However, if we are to rely on science as the arbiter of knowledge rather than ancient superstitions, the opposite conclusion is warranted. Evolution removes the need to introduce God at any step in the process of the development of life from the simplest earlier forms. It does not explain the origin of life, so this gap still remains. This is insufficient to maintain the consistency for some believers, especially since evolution

---

[31] Stenger, *God, The Failed Hypothesis*, 50.

is in deep disagreement with the biblical narrative of simultaneously created immutable forms. Furthermore, we have no reason to conclude that life itself could not have had a purely material origin.[32]

Thus, Stenger admits that science has no explanation for the origin of life on earth. There is no empirical evidence that simple life forms came into existence from nonliving materials. This lack of an explanation and the lack of empirical evidence does not prove that God exists, but is certainly sufficient to suggest that God *may* exist (item 4), at least until science can clearly demonstrate that living cells can be created from nonliving materials. Even if science could create living cells from nonliving materials, this would not prove that God does not exist.

Using Stenger's approach, we could prove that intelligent life does not exist anywhere else in the universe. Consider the following argument.

1. Hypothesize that intelligent life exists elsewhere in the universe.
2. Assume that intelligent life is capable of making its presence known beyond its local habitation.
3. Look for evidence that there is intelligent life elsewhere in the universe with an open mind.
4. If such evidence is found, conclude that intelligent life *may* exist elsewhere in the universe.
5. If no such evidence is found, conclude beyond a reasonable doubt that intelligent life does *not* exist elsewhere in the universe.

There is no publicly available evidence that extraterrestrial life forms exist. Thus, using Stenger's argument, we have proven that there is no intelligent life elsewhere in the universe. However, the above argument does not prove that there is no intelligent life elsewhere in the universe any more than Stenger's argument proves that God does not exist.

---

[32] Stenger, *God, The Failed Hypothesis*, 52.

Rather than attempting to prove or disprove the existence of God, in chapter 3 this question is transformed into a proposition and some of the consequences of its possible truth values are discussed. If Proposition 1 is true, then this result leads to additional propositions. Some of the consequences of their truth values are also discussed.

3

Propositions, Truth Values, and Consequences

The first question raised in Chapter 1 was: Does God exist? This question can be transformed into a proposition. Two important requirements for a proposition are:

i.   It must be clear and
ii. It must be unambiguous

Therefore, one challenge in converting Question 1 into a clear, unambiguous proposition is the use of the word 'God'. Because there are many interpretations and understandings of God, the first question is transformed into the following proposition:

Proposition 1: An infinite, intelligent entity (IIE) exists.

Before considering some of the consequences of the two possible truth values for Proposition 1, it is necessary to come to grips with the following facts. Humans are finite creatures. Everything in our human experience is finite. An IIE is not finite. Finite creatures cannot understand the infinite. They cannot approximate the infinite. Thus, there is no possible way for human beings to proceed beyond a severely limited, superficial understanding of an IIE. Second, even if humans were able to more fully comprehend characteristics of an IIE, our language limits our ability to communicate that information. Third, our culture impacts our presuppositions and our approach to obtaining a more complete understanding of concepts foreign to our own experience.

In the context of Proposition 1, an infinite, intelligent entity is a living entity that had no beginning and has no end. The entity has always existed, and the entity will always continue to exist. Second, the word infinite also refers to the powers or capabilities of such an entity. In this context there is nothing that the entity does not know, and there is nothing the entity cannot accomplish.

It is important to understand that what a person believes to be the truth value of Proposition 1 has no impact on its actual truth value. However, the truth value of Proposition 1, coupled with a person's belief about its truth value, may have a significant impact on how that person lives, and possibly on what happens when that person dies.

First, consider some of the consequences if Proposition 1 is false.

Consequences if an IIE does not exist

If Proposition 1 is false, then there is no Infinite, Intelligent Entity. The consequences of Proposition 1 being false are divided into three categories:

    i.   Impact on the origin of life on earth
    ii. Impact on world religions
    iii. Impact on individuals

Impact on the origin of life on earth

If Proposition 1 is false, then the second question raised at the beginning of chapter 1 is also answered. If no living entity has always existed, then at some point in the history of the universe, simple life forms came into existence from non-living materials. There was no Creator. There was no Intelligent Designer. Simple life forms came into existence through some inexplicable (at present) mechanism, and flourished. Over a long period of time, probably billions of years, those simple life forms evolved into life as we know it today through natural selection and modified descent. Humankind is merely an accident of nature. The explanations proposed by Unguided Evolutionists are probably correct in their attempt to explain how life on earth has evolved into its current state.

Impact on world religions

All religions that assert that their god is a supernatural being of any kind are false. In particular, Christianity, Judaism, and Islam are man-made myths. The Bible is fictitious except possibly in some of its historical narratives. Israel was not a chosen nation because there was no one to choose it. Old Testament prophets misled the Israelites and were not divinely inspired. Jesus, as described in the New Testament, did not exist. The spread of Christianity by the early apostles was based on a lie. No prayer has ever been answered, because there is no one to answer prayer.

Impact on individuals

All moral authority is based on tradition, majority opinion, or cultural norms. There is no higher moral authority to whom people must answer. Human beings, like all other living creatures, have no soul. Ultimately, it makes no difference if a person believes in an IIE or not because all humankind will suffer the same fate. Altruistic behavior, which is an integral part of Christianity as well as other religions might make a person feel better in this life, but such behavior has no eternal consequences. People have every incentive to get as much as possible for themselves since for anything they do or don't do there are only temporal and no eternal consequences. Indeed, if an IIE does not exist, then there is no reason for an individual not to look at life from a purely self-interest perspective.

The consequences of Proposition 1 being false are consistent with the statements made by Unguided Evolutionists. Life in a universe without an IIE was aptly described by Macbeth when he was informed that the queen, Lady Macbeth, was dead.

> Out, out, brief candle! Life's but a walking shadow. A poor player who struts and frets his hour upon the stage And then is heard no more. It is a tale, Told by an Idiot, full of sound and fury, Signifying nothing.[1]

---

[1]   William Shakespeare, *Macbeth*, Act V, Scene V

Thus, if Proposition 1 is false, then this path leads to a dead end!

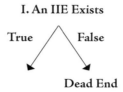

I. An IIE Exists

True　　　False

Dead End

Consequences if an IIE does exist

If Proposition 1 is true and an Infinite Intelligent Entity exists, then our curiosity is fully awakened, and we want to know more about this entity. Richard Dawkins has provided us with his thoughts about the nature of an IIE.

> The God of the Old Testament is arguably the most unpleasant character in all fiction: jealous and proud of it; a petty, unjust, unforgiving control-freak; a vindictive, bloodthirsty ethnic cleanser; a misogynistic, homophobic, racist, infanticidal, genocidal, filicidal, pestilential, megalomaniacal, sadomasochistic, capriciously malevolent bully.[2]

In contrast to Dawkins' analysis, the nature of the IIE can be explored by considering additional propositions. The second question raised in Chapter 1 asks:

What is the origin of life on earth, and in particular, human life? This question can be transformed into the following proposition.

Proposition 2: The Infinite Intelligent Entity created life on earth, including human life.

First, consider some of the consequences if Proposition 2 is false.

---

[2]　Dawkins, *The God Delusion*, 51.

Consequences if the IIE did not create life on earth

If Proposition 1 is true and Proposition 2 is false, then an Infinite Intelligent Entity exists, but that entity had no role in the creation of life on earth, and in particular, human life.

That Proposition 2 is false seems highly unlikely if the IIE exists. Nevertheless, the consequences of Proposition 2 being false need to be examined. If Proposition 2 is false, then the most obvious conclusion is that the consequences are similar to the case in which Proposition 1 is false. If the IIE had no role in the creation of life on earth, then at some point in the history of the universe, simple life forms came into existence on earth from non-living materials. There was no Creator. There was no Intelligent Designer. Simple life forms came into existence through some inexplicable mechanism and flourished. Over a long period of time those simple life forms evolved into life as we know it today through natural selection and modified descent. Humankind is an accident of nature. The Unguided Evolutionist explanations are probably correct in their attempt to explain how life has evolved to its current state.

If Proposition 2 is false, then there is no inherent relationship between humankind and the IIE. It is likely that there has been little or no communication between humankind and the IIE. There is no higher moral authority. There is no reason for an individual not to attempt to get as much as possible for himself or herself because actions have only temporal and no eternal consequences. Thus the universe is not that much different from the universe in which an IIE does not exist. This result also leads to a dead end!

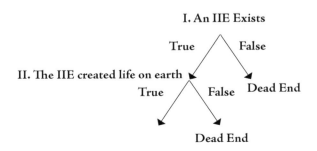

Consequences if the IIE created life on earth

If Propositions 1 and 2 are both true—there is an infinite, intelligent entity and that entity created life on earth including human life—then it is clear that we live in a totally different universe than if either proposition is false. Note that Proposition 2 makes no distinction as to whether the creation event occurred in six twenty-four hour days or over millions of years, was the product of an Intelligent Designer, or was the result of an evolutionary process guided by the IIE. While the details of how life began and how life evolved into its current state are of great interest, they are irrelevant when examining some of the consequences of Propositions 1 and 2 both being true.

If Propositions 1 and 2 are true, then this leads to a third proposition:

Proposition 3: There is life after death.

First, consider some of the consequences if Proposition 3 is false.

Consequences if there is no life after death

If Propositions 1 and 2 are true but Proposition 3 is false, then there is no life after death. If there is no life after death, then all religions that affirm life after death are mistaken. In particular, Christianity, Judaism, and Islam are wrong. Any teachings about life after death are fiction, which raises questions about the accuracy of all other descriptions of the IIE relative to those religious traditions and the source of their beliefs including the Bible and the Qur'an.

If there is no life after death, then that leads to a number of interesting questions: Why did the IIE create life, and in particular, human life, in the first place? If there is no life after death, then what is our relationship to the IIE? Is it possible to communicate with the IIE? Is it possible to develop some kind of relationship with the IIE? Why would we attempt to do so? To make life on earth more pleasant? To petition the IIE to provide us with worldly riches? We are all aware of extremely devout, morally upright, good people who lead lives of intense suffering and poverty. We are also aware of particularly vile individuals who seem to enjoy many earthly pleasures. Thus, attempts to petition the IIE for earthly rewards may not be effective.

Is there a higher moral authority? What incentive is there for a person to do anything but get as much as possible for himself or herself since there are only temporal consequences and no eternal consequences for what that person does or doesn't do? Why should we not look at life on earth from a purely self-interest perspective? Once again, this path leads to a dead end!

The following diagram summarizes the results thus far.

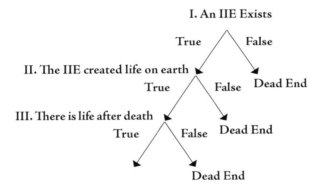

In chapter 4 some of the consequences are considered if all three Propositions are true.

4

Consequences if there is Life After Death

If an Infinite Intelligent Entity exists, if the Infinite Intelligent Entity created life on earth, and in particular human life, and if there is life after death, then life takes on new meaning.

Richard Dawkins describes an interesting argument made by Blaise Pascal:

> The great French mathematician Blaise Pascal reckoned that, however long the odds against God's existence might be, there is an even larger asymmetry in the penalty for guessing wrong. You'd better believe in God, because if you are right you stand to gain eternal bliss, and if you are wrong it won't make any difference anyway. On the other hand, if you don't believe in God and you turn out to be wrong you get eternal damnation, whereas if you are right it makes no difference. On the face of it the decision is a no-brainer. Believe in God.[1]

Christopher Hitchens has this response to Pascal:

> The ultimate degeneration of all this into a mere bargain was made unpleasantly obvious by Blaise Pascal, whose theology is not far short of the sordid. His celebrated "wager" puts it in hucksterish form: what have you got to lose? If you believe in god and there is a god, you win. If you believe in him and you are wrong—so what?

---

[1] Dawkins, *The God Delusion*, 130.

I once wrote a response to this cunning piece of bet-covering, which took two forms. The first was a version of Bertrand Russell's hypothetical reply to the hypothetical question: what will you say if you die and are confronted with your Maker? His response? "I should say, Oh God, you did not give us enough evidence." My own reply: Imponderable Sir, I presume from some if not all of your many reputations that you might prefer honest and convinced unbelief to the hypocritical and self-interested affection of faith or the smoking tributes of bloody altars. But I would not count on it.[2]

Sam Harris has this response to Pascal:

> If Christianity is correct, and I persist in my unbelief, I should expect to suffer the torments of hell. Worse still, I have persuaded others, and many close to me, to reject the very idea of God. They too will languish in "eternal fire" (Matthew 25:41). If the basic doctrine of Christianity is correct, I have misused my life in the worst conceivable way. I admit this without a single caveat. The fact that my continuous and public rejection of Christianity does not worry me in the least should suggest to you just how inadequate I think your reasons for being a Christian are.[3]

> If the basic tenets of Christianity are true, then there are some very grim surprises in store for nonbelievers like myself. You understand this. At least half of the American population understands this. So let us be honest with ourselves: in the fullness of time, one side is really going to win this argument, and the other side is really going to lose.[4]

---

[2] Hitchens, *god is not Great*, 211-212.
[3] Harris, *Letter to a Christian Nation*, 3-4.
[4] Harris, *Letter to a Christian Nation*,.5.

Is it possible that Hitchens and Harris are simply not looking in the right places for answers to their questions?

Pascal raises an interesting philosophical question: What are the consequences for making the "right decision" for the "wrong reason"? Hitchens and Harris raise a second philosophical question: What are the consequences for making the "wrong decision" for what one assumes to be the "right reason"?

If an Infinite Intelligent Entity exists, if the Infinite Intelligent Entity created life on earth, and in particular human life, and if there is life after death, then a relationship with the IIE becomes far more important because the relationship a person has with the IIE may have a profound impact on what happens in that person's life and on what happens to that person when he or she dies. Sam Harris weighs in with his thoughts concerning a relationship between an individual and the IIE.

> There is, in fact, no worldview more reprehensible in its arrogance than that of a religious believer: *the creator of the universe takes an interest in me, approves of me, loves me, and will reward me after death; my current beliefs, drawn from scripture, will remain the best statement of the truth until the end of the world; everyone who disagrees with me will spend eternity in hell.*...An average Christian in an average church, listening to an average Sunday sermon has achieved a level of arrogance simply unimaginable in scientific discourse—and there have been some extraordinarily arrogant scientists.[5]

After spending more than 20 years at one of our nation's most prestigious national laboratories, I can certainly attest to the existence of some extraordinarily arrogant scientists. At the same time, it is fascinating that Harris contends it is the height of arrogance for Christians to believe it is possible to have a relationship with the IIE who created life on earth, and in particular human life.

---

[5]   Harris, *Letter to a Christian Nation*, 74-75.

Harris also comments on topics that he believes should have been included in the Bible.

> But just imagine how breathtakingly specific a work of prophecy would be, if it were actually the product of omniscience. If the Bible were such a book, it would make perfectly accurate predictions about human events. You would expect it to contain a passage such as "In the latter half of the twentieth century, humankind will develop a globally linked system of computers—the principles of which I set forth in Leviticus—and this system shall be called the Internet." The Bible contains nothing like this. In fact, it does not contain a single sentence that could not have been written by a man or woman living in the first century. This should trouble you.
>
> A book written by an omniscient being could contain a chapter on mathematics that, after two thousand years of continuous use, would still be the richest source of mathematical insight humanity has ever known.[6]
>
> Why doesn't the Bible say anything about electricity, or about DNA, or about the actual age and size of the universe? What about a cure for cancer? When we fully understand the biology of cancer, this understanding will be easily summarized in a few pages of text. Why aren't these pages, or anything remotely like them, found in the Bible?[7]

Harris raises an interesting question. What was the IIE's purpose in providing us with the Bible? Was the purpose to impress us with scientific knowledge far beyond the capabilities of those who lived thousands of years ago? Was it to provide scientific proof for His existence? Or was the IIE's purpose to provide us with information about who God is, why God created humankind, the desired relationship between the Creator

---

[6]   Harris, *Letter to a Christian Nation*, 60.
[7]   Harris, *Letter to a Christian Nation*, 61-62.

and His creation, there is life after death; and how we can spend eternity in the presence of our Creator?

Lecturing God on what should be contained in the Bible is far more arrogant than Christians believing it is possible to have a personal relationship with God who created life on earth in the first place.

If an IIE exists, if the IIE created life on earth including human life, and if there is life after death, then this leads to a fourth proposition:

Proposition 4: Jesus, the Son of God as described in the New Testament, was a living being who came to earth approximately 2,000 years ago.

Before examining the consequences of the truth values of this proposition, it is necessary to clarify what is meant by the statement: 'Jesus, the Son of God as described in the New Testament'.

1.   Jesus was the Son of God, the IIE who created life on earth, including human life. That is, Jesus was the incarnation of God in human form. Jesus was, at the same time, fully God and fully human.
2.   Jesus was a teacher who taught people about God and how to live in accordance with the commandments and will of God.
3.   Jesus lived a life in complete harmony with God. That is, Jesus did not sin.
4.   Jesus was crucified, and three days later, he rose from the dead.
5.   By dying on the cross and rising again Jesus paid the price for our sins. As a result, we have an opportunity to spend eternity in the magnificent presence of our Creator after we die.

In response to these propositions Christopher Hitchens declares:.

> The best argument I know for the highly questionable existence of Jesus is this. His illiterate living disciples

left us no record and in any event could not have been "Christians," since they were never to read those later books in which Christians must affirm belief, and in any case had no idea that anyone would ever found a church on their master's announcements.[8]

If Propositions 1–3 are true, we have now reached a critical fork in the road relative to the viability of Christianity. In the words of the great philosopher, Yankee catcher and manager, Yogi Berra, "When you come to a fork in the road, take it."

If Proposition 4 is false, that is, Jesus as described in the New Testament did not exist, then Christianity is not a viable religion. Other religions affirm a belief in an IIE, that the IIE created life on earth, and that there is life after death. Some of these religions acknowledge that Jesus lived, but they deny that he is the Son of God and insist instead that he was merely a prophet. It is possible that one or more of these non-Christian religions may provide a reasonably accurate understanding of the IIE and the relationship of the IIE with human beings. It is also possible that none of these religions has an accurate description or understanding of the IIE. It suffices to say that in this situation, Christianity is not a valid religion and leave open the question of the true nature of the IIE and which, if any, of these religions represent the true nature of the IIE. The bottom line in the words of Pastor Kent Chevalier is: Either Jesus is the Lord of all, or not lord at all.

The possible truth values of Propositions 1–4 and their consequences are summarized in the following diagram.

---

8   Hitchens, *god is Not Great*, 114.

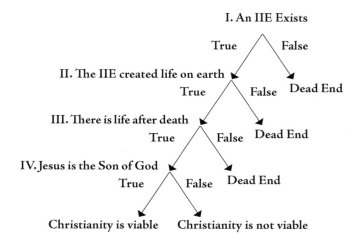

For the remainder of this book we assume that all four Propositions are true. That is, we assume that an Infinite Intelligent Entity exists, that entity created life on earth and in particular human life, there is life after death, and Jesus, the Son of God as described in the New Testament, lived some 2,000 years ago. Evidence that all four propositions are true is presented in Chapter 5.

5

God Exists and is Active in the World Today

If Propositions 1-4 are true, then it is reasonable to assume that the IIE—who we shall refer to as God—would provide some means for humankind to become aware of His existence, the relationship He desires to have with humankind, how humans should live, and what life after death entails. Because Jesus, who lived 2,000 years ago, is central to the New Testament, and the Bible is the primary source of information about God, the Bible gains instant credibility. It provides us with a basis for understanding the nature and will of God, the desired relationship between God and humankind, the role of Jesus, how we should live, and information about life after death.

As noted in Chapter 2, Victor Stenger in *God, The Failed Hypothesis*, claims to have proven that God does not exist. We have shown that his argument falls far short of a valid, scientific proof that God does not exist. At the same time, there is no universally agreed upon scientific proof that God does exist.

Sam Harris weighs in with his comments concerning evidence that God exists.

> While believing strongly, without evidence, is considered a mark of madness or stupidity in any other area of our lives, faith in God still holds immense prestige in our society. Religion is the one area of our discourse where it is considered noble to pretend to be certain about things no human being could possibly be certain about. It is

telling that this aura of nobility extends only to those faiths that still have many subscribers.[1]

In contrast to Harris, Stenger, and other Unguided Evolutionists, I believe that there is significant evidence that God does exist and that God is active in the world today, although the supporting evidence may not rise to the level of scientific proof. However, there is both indirect and direct evidence supporting these claims.

Life Exists

There is no provable scientific explanation for the origin of life on earth. Science has been unable to create living cells from nonliving materials even under tightly controlled conditions. Thus, there is no scientific evidence that living cells came into existence from nonliving materials under natural circumstances. Furthermore, as noted in chapter 1, there are only conjectures concerning how more complex life forms came into existence. One possible solution to this dilemma is that God created life on earth. Whether intelligent life evolved through some combination of Creationism, Intelligent Design, or Guided Evolution—although a truly fascinating question—is not relevant to the truth value of Proposition 1.

The Incredible Universe

The Copernican Principle, also known as the Principle of Mediocrity or the Principle of Indifference, states that there is nothing particularly special about the earth. Earth is described as a typical planet orbiting a typical star in a more or less homogeneous universe. This view is often accompanied by the more philosophical statement that the material world is all that exists, and there is no underlying purpose for its existence. If these statements are true, then one would expect to find a universe teeming with life due to the incredible number of stars in our galaxy and the incredible number of galaxies in the universe.

---

[1] Harris, *Letter to a Christian Nation*, 67-68.

Frank Drake and Carl Sagan believed that intelligent life is quite common in the Milky Way galaxy and elsewhere in the universe.

> Using the best available estimates at the time, Drake and Sagan arrived at a startling conclusion: intelligent life should be common and widespread throughout the galaxy. In fact, Carl Sagan estimated in 1974 that a million civilizations may exist in our Milky Way galaxy alone. Given that our galaxy is but one of hundreds of billions of galaxies in the Universe, the number of intelligent alien species would then be enormous.[2]

The validity of this statement depends upon two assumptions:

 i. Living cells came into existence from nonliving materials.
 ii. More complex life forms evolved from simple life forms.

These assumptions are similar to the assumptions that Unguided Evolutionists believe happened on earth.

However, Peter Ward and Donald Brownlee argue that:

> ... not only intelligent life, but even the simplest of animal life, is exceedingly rare in our galaxy and in the Universe. We are not saying that life is rare, only animal life is.[3]

Ward and Brownlee identify some of the factors necessary to support animal life which include:

 1. The planet must be the right distance from the star.
 2. The star must have the proper mass.
 3. There must be planets nearby that can protect the planet containing animal life from destruction by comets and asteroids.

---

[2] Peter D. Ward and Donald Brownlee, *Rare Earth*, (New York: Copernicus, 2000), xiv.
[3] Ward and Brownlee, *Rare Earth*, xiv.

4. The orbits of the planets must be stable.
5. The other planets orbiting the star must have the right mass.
6. There must be plate tectonics on the planet to enhance biotic diversity.
7. Oceans must exist.
8. There must be a large moon to stabilize the tilt of the axis of rotation.
9. The tilt must fall in a reasonably small range so the seasons will not be too severe.
10. The proper amount of carbon must be present.
11. The atmosphere must be able to maintain an appropriate temperature, pressure, and composition.
12. There must be an evolutionary pathway to produce complex plants and animal life.
13. The galaxy must contain enough heavy elements, should not be too small, elliptical or irregular.
14. The star must be in the right position in the galaxy, not in the center nor on the edge.[4]

After assessing the odds that all of the above requirements were satisfied, along with certain additional requirements, Ward and Brownlee conclude:

> Years from now, after the astrobiology revolution has matured, our understanding of the various factors that have allowed animal life to develop on this planet will be much greater than it is now. Many new factors will be known, and the list of variables involved will undoubtedly be amended. But it is our contention that any strong signal can be perceived even when only sparse data are available. To us, the signal is so strong that even at this time, it appears that Earth indeed may be extraordinarily rare.[5]

In his book, *The Creator and the Cosmos* (1993), Hugh Ross provides a list of parameters whose values must lie in a very small range in order for

---

4   Ward and Brownlee, *Rare Earth*, xxvii-xxviii.
5   Ward and Brownlee, *Rare Earth*, 275.

any form of life to exist. He estimates the probability that all 128 of these parameters lie within the prescribed narrow limits is 10^{-166}.

To put this number in perspective, consider the following illustration. The Powerball Lottery involves picking 5 numbers from 1–59, and then picking 1 number from 1–39. To win the jackpot, typically worth tens or hundreds of millions of dollars, you must pick all six of these numbers correctly. If you purchase one ticket, the probability of picking all six numbers correctly is $1/195,249,054 \approx 0.0000000051$. If Ross's analysis is correct, the probability of a planet with all 128 parameters lying within the prescribed narrow ranges is approximately the same as the probability of winning the Powerball Jackpot twenty times by purchasing only one ticket each time. Ross also estimates that the total number of planets in the universe is about 10^{22}. If that estimate is accurate, then the probability that a planet exists with all 128 parameters lying within the prescribed narrow ranges is about 10^{-144}. In order to match that probability a person would need to win the Powerball Jackpot approximately 17 times. If a person won the Powerball jackpot twice, let alone 17 times, would anyone believe it was just coincidence?

It is interesting that Unguided Evolutionists often rail against Christians for their intolerance of those who disagree with them as seen in the following assertion by Richard Dawkins.

> This ambition to achieve what can only be called a Christian fascist state is entirely typical of the American Taliban. It is an almost exact mirror image of the Islamic fascist state so ardently sought by many people in other parts of the world.[6]

On the other hand, Ben Stein, in his documentary, *Expelled, No Intelligence Allowed*, provided several examples of the intolerance of some scientists toward those who do not believe that Unguided Evolution is a scientific fact. One of the victims of this intolerance was Dr. Guillermo Gonzalez, who appears in the movie. He was denied tenure at Iowa State University despite the fact that his book, *The Privileged Planet: How our*

---

[6] Dawkins, *The God Delusion*, 330-331.

Place in the Cosmos is Designed for Discovery, was peer reviewed prior to its publication and includes some very favorable comments for its scientific accuracy and thought-provoking analysis. The examples contained in this documentary are but a tiny fraction of the examples of such intolerance practiced by a number of Unguided Evolutionists toward those who disagree with their beliefs.

Gonzalez and Jay Richards quote the Russian physicist Lev Landau about cosmologists.

Cosmologists are often wrong, but never in doubt.[7]

The same can be said about Unguided Evolutionists.

The Rapid Spread of Christianity After Jesus' Death

Many atheists claim that no independent sources corroborate the contents of the Bible, and in particular, the gospels and Acts. As a result, they claim the Bible cannot be believed. Before addressing those claims it must be noted that most historians generally agree about certain facts. First, in the years shortly after the time period when Christians believe Jesus lived, died, and rose again, a dramatic cultural shift occurred among the Jews. In particular, the followers of Jesus changed or abandoned five social structures and practices that had been a part of their culture and religious beliefs for hundreds of years. These practices were:

1. The annual sacrifices of animals as atonement for their sins.
2. The belief that what separated them from the pagans was obedience to the laws that God had given to Moses. This belief changed when they concluded that obedience to those laws alone does not enable one to be an upstanding member of the community.

---

7   Guillermo Gonzalez and Jay Richards, *The Privileged Planet*, (Washington: Regnery, 2004), 247.

3. For well over a thousand years they believed that only religious devotion should be practiced on the Sabbath which was celebrated on Saturday. The early Christians began to worship on Sunday because it was the day that Jesus rose from the dead.

4. Prior to Jesus the Jews believed in one God, not the triune God consisting of the Father, the Son, and the Holy Spirit. The belief in the Father, Son, and Holy Spirit was radically different and would have been heresy among the Jews.

5. The early Christians believed that the Messiah suffered and died to atone for their sin. Prior to that time the Jews believed that the Messiah would deliver them from Roman oppression.

These cultural changes occurred in a very short period of time.

> How can you possibly explain why in a short period of time not just one Jew but an entire community of at least ten thousand Jews were willing to give up these five key practices that had served them sociologically and theologically for so many centuries? My explanation is simple: they had seen Jesus risen from the dead.[8]

The life, death, resurrection and the belief that Jesus was the Son of God is the only logical explanation for these major cultural changes.

> When a major cultural shift takes place, historians always look for events that can explain it....There's no question it began shortly after the death of Jesus and spread so rapidly that within a period of maybe twenty years it had even reached Caesar's palace in Rome. Not only that, but this movement triumphed over a number of competing ideologies and eventually overwhelmed the entire Roman empire.[9]

---

[8] J. P. Moreland as quoted in Lee Strobel, *The Case for Christ* (1998) p.251
[9] J. P. Moreland, quoted in Strobel, *The Case for Christ*, p.254

Other sources also corroborate the existence of Jesus. The Jewish historian Josephus mentions both James, the brother of Jesus, and Jesus himself in his writings.

> Josephus was a very important Jewish historian from the first century. He was born in AD 37 and he wrote most of his works toward the end of the first century.[10]

> As you can imagine from his collaboration with the hated Romans, Josephus was extremely disliked by his fellow Jews. But he became very popular among Christians, because in his writing he refers to James, the brother of Jesus, and to Jesus himself.[11]

Edwin Yamauchi comments on the significance of James and Jesus being referenced by Josephus.

> Highly significant...especially since his accounts of the Jewish War have proved to be very accurate; for example, they've been corroborated through archaeological excavations at Masada as well as by historians like Tacitus. He's considered to be a pretty reliable historian, and his mentioning of Jesus is considered extremely important.[12]

Michael Martin, an atheist philosopher at Boston University, questions why Jesus was not the most important figure in Josephus' writings.

> If Jesus did exist, one would have expected Josephus to have said more about him....It is unexpected that Josephus mentioned him...in passing while mentioning other Messianic figures and John the Baptist in greater detail.[13]

---

[10] Edwin M. Yamauchi, quoted in Strobel, *The Case for Christ*, p 77
[11] Edwin M. Yamauchi, quoted in Strobel, *The Case for Christ*, p 78
[12] Edwin M. Yamauchi, quoted in Strobel, *The Case for Christ*, p.81
[13] Michael Martin, **The Case Against Christianity**, quoted in **The Case for Christ**, by Lee Strobel, p.81

Yamauchi's responds:

> ... remember, Jesus didn't even object to paying taxes to the Romans. Therefore, because Jesus and his followers didn't pose an immediate political threat, it's certainly understandable that Josephus isn't more interested in this sect—even though in hindsight it turned out to be very important indeed.[14]

Another ancient author, Tacitus, who writes about the burning of Rome in 64 AD, refers to Christ and describes the violence against the early Christians.

> Nero fastened the guilt and inflicted the most exquisite tortures on a class hated for their abominations, called Christians by the populace. Christus, from whom the name had its origin, suffered the extreme penalty during the reign of Tiberius at the hands of one of our procurators, Pontius Pilatus, and a most mischievous superstition, thus checked for the moment, again broke out not only in Judea, the first source of the evil, but also in Rome....Accordingly, an arrest was first made of all who pleaded guilty: then, upon their information, an immense multitude was convicted, not so much of the crime of firing the city, as of hatred against mankind[15].

If Jesus did not exist, or if there were no eyewitnesses to his teaching and miracles, would Christianity have spread throughout the Roman Empire? Spreading Christianity meant taking risks, enduring hardships, suffering, and even death. Would they have continued to spread Christianity if they did not believe it? Would the early Christians have suffered such persecution if Jesus did not exist and their message was known to be a lie? Consider the comments of J. P. Moreland.

---

[14] Edwin M. Yamauchi, quoted in Strobel, **The Case for Christ**, p.81
[15] Tacitus, **Annals**, quoted in Strobel, **The Case for Christ**, p.82

First, the disciples were in a unique position to know whether the Resurrection happened, and they went to their deaths proclaiming it was true. Nobody knowingly and willingly dies for a lie. Second, apart from the Resurrection, there's no good reason why skeptics like Paul and James would have been converted and would have died for their faith. Third, within weeks of the crucifixion, thousands of Jews began abandoning key social practices that had critical sociological and religious importance for centuries. They believed they risked damnation if they were wrong. Fourth, the early sacraments of Communion and baptism affirmed Jesus' resurrection and deity. And fifth, the miraculous emergence of the church in the face of brutal Roman persecution "rips a great hole in history, a hole the size and shape of Resurrection" as C. F. D. Moule put it.[16]

Ken Humphreys claims that the martyrdom of Jesus' followers is pure fabrication.

Around this non-existent godman inventive minds fabricate a gang of equally non-existent disciples. These noble fellows are accorded a colourful variety of fictitious deaths and their fanciful heroics are said to inspire generations of loving Christians who cruelly suffer persecutions at the hands of dastardly Roman emperors.

One of the reeds of straw holding up the shabby edifice of Christendom is the alleged suffering and cruel fate of his original apostles, the 12 disciples chosen by the Lord himself. By their heroic, cheek-turning sacrifice, these worthies earned their martyr's crown and joined their Lord in Heaven. In so-doing, they inspired generations of noble Christians, who ultimately taught the blood-thirsty Romans the Christian values of compassion and brotherly love. Well, that's the myth. Though cruelty and

---

[16] As quoted in Strobel, **The Case for Christ**, pp.263-264

human suffering have ever been integral to the history of the Church the fanatics of Christ have rarely been the victimized innocents. Rather it has been the Christians who have bathed their faith in the blood of others.

There is NO corroborating evidence for the existence of the 12 Apostles and absolutely NO evidence for the colorful variety of martyrs' deaths they supposedly experienced.[17]

One question that could be raised in response to Humphreys' claims is, how does the Bible compare with other ancient texts in terms of their validity and support? Benjamin Warfield, a professor at the Princeton Theological Seminary, has the following answer.

If we compare the present state of the New Testament text with that of any other ancient writing, we must ... declare it to be marvelously correct. Such has been the care with which the New Testament has been copied—a care which has doubtless grown out of true reverence for its holy words....The New Testament [is] unrivaled among ancient writing in the purity of its text as actually transmitted and kept in use.[18]

Consider the biographies of Alexander the Great which are generally accepted as being historically accurate. Dr. Craig Blomberg a Distinguished Professor of the New Testament at Denver Seminary who is considered one of the foremost authorities on the four gospels, makes the following observation.

The two earliest biographies of Alexander the Great were written by Arrian and Plutarch more than four hundred years after Alexander's death in 323 BC, yet historians consider them to be generally trustworthy. Yet, legendary

---

[17] www.jesusneverexisted.com/apostles.html
[18] As quoted in **The Case for Christ**, Strobel, p.70

material about Alexander did develop over time, but it was only in the centuries after these two writers.[19]

Blomberg is supported by Professor F. F. Bruce of the University of Manchester in England:

> There is no body of ancient literature in the world which enjoys such a wealth of good textual attestation as the New Testament.[20]

In addition, archaeological evidence strongly supports the truth of the Bible.

> Within the last hundred years archaeology has repeatedly unearthed discoveries that have confirmed specific references in the gospels, particularly the gospel of John—ironically, the one that's supposedly so suspect![21]

Christianity is Different from Other Religions

Either Christianity is a valid religion or it is a purely human invention. If Christianity was a purely human invention, chances are it would look very different, and it would contain a very different message. Human nature is about power and control—not only in matters of religion, but in political, social and all other aspects of life. Chances are there would be a supreme religious figure who would have absolute authority over all subjects. One goal of this type of religion would be world domination, and achieving world domination would be acceptable by any means necessary. Critics and competing religions would not be tolerated and would be eliminated. Those who helped to enforce the edicts of the religious authority would be promised rich rewards after their death, most likely in the form of some earthly pleasure.

---

[19] As quoted in Strobel, **The Case for Christ**, p.33
[20] As quoted in Strobel, **The Case for Christ**, p.63
[21] As quoted in Strobel, **The Case for Christ**, p.50

In contrast, Christianity is the exact opposite. Jesus emphasized humility and service. World domination is not a goal. Consider the following verses of scripture.

> But I tell you who hear me: Love your enemies, do good to those who hate you, bless those who curse you, pray for those who mistreat you. If someone strikes you on one cheek, turn to him the other also. If someone takes your cloak, do not stop him from taking your tunic. Give to everyone who asks you, and if anyone takes what belongs to you, do not demand it back. Do to others as you would have them do to you (Luke 6:27-31).

The fact that Christianity is so different from what one would expect of a religion developed entirely by human beings is indirect evidence that Christianity is not man-made, and that Jesus lived some 2000 years ago.

Personal Experiences

There are thousands if not millions of Christians who have had real life experiences which have provided evidence that God exists and is active in the world today. In this section I cite the experiences of three people that I know personally. The first two, Stephanie and Thomas, I know through my church, North Way Christian Community, which is located north of Pittsburgh in Wexford, Pennsylvania. The third person is a man named Peter whom I met through a longtime friend in Florida.

Stephanie's Story

Stephanie hosted a daily talk show on WORD FM, a Christian radio station in Pittsburgh. She was also part of the North Way worship team at both the Wexford and Oakland campuses. I got to know Stephanie from her ministry at the Wexford campus. She is an extremely talented singer, a very devout Christian, and a truly delightful person. I thoroughly appreciated her ministry as part of the worship team.

In 2007, Stephanie took some time off from being a worship leader, which at that point, was almost exclusively at the Oakland campus. One Sunday in August, Pastor Jay Passavant was in Oakland for the services there. Stephanie asked Pastor Jay if he knew why she was no longer singing with the worship team. Stephanie has enormous respect for Pastor Jay, and she was concerned that he might think she was upset about something at North Way. Stephanie wanted to assure him that was not the case.

Stephanie explained to Pastor Jay that she had visited a throat specialist several months earlier who had diagnosed her with two lesions on her vocal cords which were causing her chronic hoarseness. The doctor suggested that the lesions might go away after three or four months of therapy, and that it would be best if she stopped singing until the lesions diminished or disappeared. After several months of therapy the lesions had not diminished, and the doctor said that the only way to eliminate the lesions was through surgery. The doctor explained that this surgery involved some risk of losing her voice. Because Stephanie's job as a radio talk show host required her to use her voice on a daily basis, Stephanie and her husband decided that surgery was not a viable option. The doctor responded that Stephanie would just have to make the best of the situation.

After hearing her story Pastor Jay felt led to lay his hands on her throat and pray for healing. Stephanie desperately wanted to be healed, but she had doubts about whether his prayer would do any good.

After Pastor Jay prayed for her, Stephanie was feeling better, and she decided to test the waters by attempting to sing again. Stephanie approached the Oakland campus praise team leader, Dan Bryan, and told him that she would be available for worship if needed. Although Stephanie was feeling better when she sang, she was still holding back for fear of losing her voice.

On October 7, 2007, Stephanie attended North Way at the main campus in Wexford. A North Way member named Jean approached Stephanie after the service. Jean told Stephanie that God had told her that Stephanie was having a problem with her throat and that Jean should keep an eye on Stephanie throughout the service and pray for her. Stephanie had never met Jean prior to that day. Jean told Stephanie that God wanted to heal her, and that after she was healed, her voice would be stronger than ever. Jean put her hand on the front of Stephanie's throat and prayed. Stephanie and her husband felt God's healing presence, and they stood there with tears streaming down their faces. God had touched Stephanie, and she knew there was a reason. God had a purpose for her voice. She thanked God for her healing.

The following Sunday Stephanie received a phone call from Pastor Scott Stevens. Scott said he had been talking to Jean about what God was doing at North Way. Jean told Scott that she had been led to pray for two women at North Way, and that God was healing them. She said that God told her that the woman named Stephanie was now healed. When Scott called Stephanie, she confirmed to Scott what she had known that entire week: she had been completely healed!

After the healing Stephanie was busy with her talk show five afternoons each week. In addition, she began writing, rehearsing and recording songs on Fridays and Saturdays for an album entitled 'Shine' which was released in August, 2008. Stephanie hopes that she will be used by God to touch the hearts of others that they may glorify God.

In October, 2008, Stephanie gave a concert at North Way Wexford prior to moving to Florida. Shortly after moving to Florida Stephanie accepted a job as the host of a morning show on a Christian radio station in Fort Myers. She was eager and excited to use her talents to serve God in her new location. Stephanie has had no recurrence of the throat problems. Her miraculous healing is undeniable. In the words of Pastor Jay, "Undeniable prevails over inexplicable."

Thomas' Story

Thomas has an even more amazing story. He was raised in a Christian family just outside of Pittsburgh. While in high school and college Thomas sang and participated in theatrical productions. After graduating from college he went to New York and performed off Broadway. At the age of 35, with a wife and three children, Thomas decided to attend law school. After getting his JD degree, Thomas returned to his hometown to set up his law practice.

Thomas began having health problems in March, 2002. He began to feel pain in the right side of his face. The doctors diagnosed his condition as sialolithiasis, which is a blockage of the saliva gland. Sialolithiasis often produces intense pain in one side of the face. Thomas' pain did not go away and kept getting worse. In July 2002 Thomas underwent surgery to remove the saliva gland. It turned out that the gland was healthy and was not the cause of his suffering. After surgery the pain got much worse.

Later that year Thomas was diagnosed with trigeminal neuralgia (TN). TN is a neuropathic disorder involving facial nerves. It causes intense pain in the face and possibly other areas such as the ear, eye, lips, nose, and forehead. Kim Burchiel, a physician and professor and chairman of neurological surgery at the Oregon Health & Science University School of Medicine, treats TN patients. He says that TN patients are in total agony and often beg to be killed. TN has been called the suicide disease and is the most painful affliction known to medical practitioners.

The pain endured by TN sufferers is caused by an artery that compresses the trigeminal nerve which is located deep within the brain. The compression injures the nerve's protective myelin sheath and produces erratic and hyperactive nerve function. The result is intense pain in the area served by the nerve, and it hinders the ability of the nerve to shut off the pain signals after the stimulus to the nerve ends. Sufferers of a variant of TN, called atypical trigeminal neuralgia (ATN), may also experience an intense burning sensation. (Mayo Clinic website)

Thomas' doctors recommended microvascular decompression surgery to treat his TN. Microvascular decompression surgery involves opening a hole in the skull behind the ear and implanting a protective shield around the damaged nerve. On October 24, 2002, Thomas underwent this surgery.

The surgery did not relieve his pain, and a complication ensued. Fluid was seeping from his brain through his eyes. It was determined that the sac in the brain containing spinal fluid, which had been cut during the surgery, was not properly sealed. A spinal tap was performed to relieve the pressure. Later, his doctor decided to install a lumbar drain to collect the fluid. Neither of these procedures was successful. The doctors decided additional surgery was necessary to properly seal the sac in the brain containing the spinal fluid. This surgery involved the use of a cadaver graft to achieve the necessary seal.

After the second surgery Thomas went home, but his pain persisted. He couldn't sleep. He was simultaneously freezing cold and was covered with an oily sweat. Finally, about 3:00 AM, Thomas called the hospital. He was life-flighted to Pittsburgh where a third surgery was performed. During this surgery his heart stopped for 5 minutes and 57 seconds. According to the americanheart.org website, brain death and permanent death begin to occur in four to six minutes after experiencing cardiac arrest. Thomas was that close to dying.

After the third surgery Thomas continued to suffer from incredible pain. His right arm from halfway between the elbow and his hand felt like it was on fire. His left leg felt shattered. His right leg felt like it was pinned down. His abdomen felt like it had been blasted with a shotgun. Nerves in his brain were damaged and were sending false signals. Attempts to treat the pain were unsuccessful. His pain never left.

Because the surgeons had to stop the procedure during the third surgery in order to revive him, a fourth surgery was needed to complete the procedure. After the fourth surgery Thomas was undergoing CT scans several times a day. A pod was forming in his brain. The pod was growing and needed to be removed. A fifth surgery was required to remove the pod. After 27 days in the hospital and five surgeries, Thomas went home. He had to give himself an IV every morning and every evening. The extreme pain never went away.

Thomas went to a pain clinic in Pittsburgh in an attempt to identify possible techniques to tolerate his intense pain. Nothing helped. Thomas was told about three other men at the pain clinic who were suffering from severe head trauma and pain, but due to other causes. Two of the men committed suicide. Thomas had gone back to work, but he was in such agony that there was little he could accomplish.

Thomas had discovered that the time limit on the cadaver tissue used in the second surgery had expired prior to his surgery, so he decided to sue. He was in debt because his insurance did not cover all of the treatment he had received. Thomas was not trying to get rich, he was just trying to pay his bills and have enough money for his family to live.

Thomas had been attending North Way. After he became ill, Thomas talked to Pastor Jay many times, and they often prayed together seeking relief from his intense pain. Thomas read books on healing. He looked for a common denominator for the healing described in the Bible, but found none. He prayed earnestly for God to remove this pain, but the pain persisted. He gained comfort by reading the 9th chapter of the Gospel of John which talked about Jesus performing healings to glorify God. Thomas prayed that he would be healed to glorify God.

For 15 months Thomas endured a life of constant, intense pain. He continued to give himself an IV each morning and each evening, but his pain never diminished.

On Friday, January 30, 2004, Thomas' sixteen year old son asked his father if they could go to the Refiner's Fire service at North Way that evening. Thomas begged off because he just didn't feel up to it. His son persisted. Thomas reluctantly agreed to go.

The service began at 7:00 PM and was scheduled to go until about 8:30 PM. Because Thomas had to give himself an IV after work, and they had over a 30 minute drive to North Way, Thomas and his son did not arrive until 7:15. The worship center was nearly filled with about 1200 people, so Thomas and his son sat in the back. The theme of the Refiner's Fire was healing, but Thomas had no thought of being healed that night.

The service did not end at 8:30 but continued until almost 9:00 PM. Near the end of the service Pastor Jay prayed for healing for those in the audience who were suffering. During that prayer, something truly amazing happened. Suddenly, Thomas felt the pain being lifted from his body. He was standing at the time and was afraid to move. His initial reaction was that he finally found a position that would provide some relief from the pain. Thomas turned to his son and said, "The pain is gone." His son said, "You've been healed." Thomas and his son both started to cry.

Thomas wanted to share the good news with Pastor Jay. He walked to the front of the worship center, but unbeknownst to him, Pastor Jay had migrated to the back while a few people had taken a roving microphone to tell how they had been healed. Thomas looked back at his son who motioned to him that Pastor Jay was in the back of the worship center. Thomas went to the back to talk to Pastor Jay. They both went into the lobby where Thomas told Pastor Jay the good news.

Thomas didn't know what to do. He left the building for a moment, then returned to be with his son. Pastor Jay went to the front of the worship center and announced that a miraculous healing had taken place. He invited Thomas to come forward to tell his story. Thomas went down front and briefly told his story. Pastor Jay then asked Thomas what he wanted to do. Thomas said, "I want to scream." And he did. Then Thomas said he wanted to run back to his seat, an act which would have been impossible just minutes earlier. And he did.

I was at the Refiner's Fire Service that night and witnessed this healing. It was a night that everyone who attended will never forget. God's presence was palpable. Thomas' miraculous cure is undeniable. There is no medical explanation for how he was healed. Since that night Thomas has had no recurrence of the pain from TN. Once again, undeniable prevails over inexplicable.

Peter's Story

Few if any of us can even begin to imagine the overwhelming fear, danger, despair and utter hopelessness that Peter and his family faced when Peter was a child. Peter was born in July, 1964 in a small village in Mozambique, Africa. At the time of his birth Mozambique was a colony of Portugal. In September, 1964, the Front for the Liberation of Mozambique (FRELIMO) began a war of independence. As the fight for independence gained momentum, citizens of Mozambique were rounded up by Portuguese forces and placed in concentration camps. In order to avoid this fate many families fled into the bush and joined the FRELIMO freedom fighters.

When Peter was about three years old, the war for independence spread to his village. Peter's father joined the FRELIMO freedom fighters. Peter, his mother, two older brothers and an older sister, along with most of the families from the village, fled from their homes to take refuge in the bush. Families dug small holes in the ground to provide shelter and minimal protection from the elements and from leopards, lions, and hyenas who called the bush home. The holes also provided primitive hiding places in an attempt to avoid discovery by Portuguese soldiers who roamed the area. Food was scarce. Disease was prevalent. In the evening when the temperature dropped, there were no blankets to help people keep warm. Open fires were not permitted because they could be spotted from the air and bombs would be dropped on the encampment. Death was a constant companion. Dead bodies were never buried but were left for wild animals to consume. When Portuguese soldiers approached the camp, families fled and scattered into the bush. Sometimes children were separated from parents never to be seen again.

After living in the bush for more than four years, Peter's father decided to flee from the freedom fighters and go to the Portuguese concentration camp where he thought life would be more bearable. Leaving the FRELIMO camp was dangerous. The FRELIMO militia attempted to prevent families from leaving because family members knew the location of the FRELIMO camp, and if they were captured by Portuguese soldiers, they would be tortured until they revealed the camp's location. Fortunately, Peter's family successfully left the camp, and made it to the concentration camp without incident.

Some of the refugees in the concentration camp were permitted to work in the nearby fields to gather food. However, if the refugees failed to return or were caught collaborating with the FRELIMO, family members were punished or even killed. Peter and his family endured the grim reality of the concentration camp for another four years.

Finally, after ten long years of war, a cease-fire was signed in September, 1974. Mozambique formally gained its independence from Portugal on

June 25, 1975. For the first eleven years of his life all Peter knew was war, poverty, starvation, disease, and death. Finally, at age eleven, Peter and his family were able to leave the concentration camp, and Peter was able to attend school for the first time in his life. The language spoken at the school was Portuguese.

After Mozambique finally gained its independence, the leader of FRELIMO, Samoral Moises Machel, was elected president. President Machel immediately brought communists into the government and promptly closed all of the churches. The word "God" was never mentioned, and there were no bibles in any of the schools.

In 1978 after completing the 4th grade, Peter's family could no longer afford to send him to school. Peter left home and went to the town of Chimoio to find work. The only work he could find was washing plates and cleaning houses.

In 1977 a violent civil war had erupted as the Mozambique National Resistance (RENAMO) rebelled against the Marxist government. The FRELIMO government forced every boy and girl to join the government forces against the RENAMO. While living in Chimoio Peter was taken into custody by government operatives to force him to join the FRELIMO war effort. However, because Peter was blind in his right eye from a disease contracted shortly after birth, each time he was arrested he was later released. The government determined that Peter was incapable of firing a weapon because of his handicap. After his third arrest and release, Peter decided to return home to his family.

The FRELIMO government soon imposed a new edict which required every male from age 10 to 45 to go to join the war effort. Thus, Peter would no longer be exempt from fighting. Peter's mother told him to leave the country at once and seek refuge in neighboring Zimbabwe. Peter's mother prepared a meal and put it in a clay jar. This act was more than just giving Peter food for his journey. It was a symbolic way of saying goodbye to a family member who might never be seen again. When the food ran out, it was very possible that Peter would die. It was an emotional and extremely difficult goodbye for Peter and his family. His mother hoped that Peter and his family would be reunited in the spirit world.

So, at age fifteen, Peter left his home and his family to travel through the bush to migrate to a land where he could not speak the language and where he would be a border jumper with no passport, no official papers, no money, and where he would be living illegally. His journey through the bush was fraught with danger from wild animals, land mines, and soldiers who searched the bush for anyone attempting to flee the country. After a three-day journey Peter reached the Kairezi River which formed the border between Zimbabwe and Mozambique.

Now Peter was confronted with a new problem. He could not swim across the river because it was home to crocodiles and other predators. Also, soldiers patrolled the river banks, and if a person was caught crossing into Zimbabwe without the proper papers, he was either sent back to the FRELIMO soldiers or shot. The only way to cross the river was to pay smugglers to transport people between 2:00 and 4:00 AM in crude canoes made from tree skins. Peter had no money, but someone—to this day he does not know who—paid his fee, and he successfully migrated to Zimbabwe.

Peter had an uncle in the Katerere area of Zimbabwe, and he sought refuge in his uncle's house. However, his uncle refused to take him in which violated a cultural norm. Fortunately, Peter found work tending cattle and goats and plowing fields. Each day he awakened early in the morning and took the animals through the jungle to the fields which were several miles away. He returned home with the animals about 6:30 or 7:00 PM. Early in his stay, he was whipped when he made a mistake, but as time went on he became a trusted and valued employee.

In November, 1980, Peter had a vision that changed his life. In the vision he saw Jesus standing on a mountain. When Jesus stepped onto the earth, the mountain split into two pieces between his feet. In the center was a pool of water, and all humanity was in the pool. After a short time the pool of water turned into a pool of fire and a great cry arose from people who were suffering. Peter saw himself in the pool, and he had never felt such intense pain. He cried out in agony. Suddenly, an angel of the Lord appeared to him and commanded Peter to listen to the words of Jesus. Jesus told Peter that He was sending him to help others. Then the angel lifted Peter out of the fire.

Peter was unable to understand the vision because he had never been in church and had never heard of the Bible. Until this point in his life Peter's only exposure to religion involved ancestor worship through which men were challenged to make their grandfathers and great grandfathers proud of them. In difficult times they believed the spirits were angry with them. Beer drinking, which was also a part of ancestral worship, was a nightly occurrence for adults in an effort to escape the grim realities of famine, disease, and death.

Peter began to have other visions in his dreams at night. The visions were like a giant puzzle that was being revealed piece by piece, but he did not understand their meaning. In one vision he was told by a man that the spirit of the Lord was on him and that the Lord wanted to use him. However, Peter had no idea what the man meant.

After taking care of the cattle and goats for nearly two years, the Lord again spoke to Peter, telling him to go to Harare, which is the capital of Zimbabwe. When Peter told his employers of his desire to leave, they tried to talk him out of it. He was a valued employee, and they wanted him to stay. Peter had no shoes and had never been to a big city. He had no promise of a job, and no way to get to Harare.

In another vision God told Peter that He would provide for him. God told him that he would meet a man who was an unbeliever, and he was to talk to him about the Lord Jesus Christ. Within days a man arrived who said he had planned to go to Harare. Peter recognized him as the man in his vision, and he began to talk to him. At first the man resisted, but later the man became a believer. Peter asked if he could accompany him to Harare, and the man agreed. After training his successor Peter was able to leave for Harare with this man.

Peter arrived in Harare in June, 1982 and found a job working with Christians in exchange for food, accommodations, and a small amount of money. Over the next two years Peter began to worship in a local church where he learned about the Lord Jesus Christ. During that time some of the puzzle pieces that he had accumulated through his earlier visions started to make sense to him because they related to passages in the Bible.

In 1984 God again spoke to Peter in a vision. This time God told him to go to the Bible College (now known as Living Waters Bible College) in Harare. After sharing his vision with some of the people he knew in Harare, they told him this was not a message from God. He did not have the background to enter the college. He had only a fourth grade education, and he did not speak English which was the language spoken at the college.

Over the previous two years Peter had managed to save enough money to cover tuition, but he could not afford the other essentials. As part of the application process, the Bible College required documentation that he would be supported by the church elders, but the elders refused to sign those documents. In their view, he was not qualified to attend the Bible College, and they did everything in their power to discourage him from doing so. Peter could not even complete the application for admission because he could not write in English.

Over the next few months Peter temporarily abandoned his efforts to attend the Bible College. One night during his prayer time a stranger knocked on the door of the small, two-room dwelling Peter called home. Peter opened the door, and the stranger asked him if he needed help on something. Peter explained that he wanted to go to the Bible College, but he needed to complete the application in English, a language he did not understand. The stranger asked Peter for some paper, and he wrote the words necessary for Peter to complete the application. Peter then copied the words the man had written and took the completed application to the Bible College in person. Peter never saw the stranger again.

When Peter arrived at the Bible College, he met with the Deans and other administrators. He asked for an interpreter because he could not speak English. This request confused his interviewers because Peter had given them his application which had been written in English. Peter told them how the application had been completed, and he shared with them some of his visions. Initially, the administrators opposed his admission because they did not believe he was qualified. Finally, an American administrator, Dr. G. Rozel, came to his support, suggesting that if God was truly directing Peter to attend the Bible College, then they would see God's work in his studies. In the end, the administrators agreed to admit him.

Peter was admitted in November, 1985, and classes for the next term began in the second week of January, 1986. In the time between his acceptance and when classes were to start, Peter returned to his church in Harare. While there he began to question his decision to enter the Bible College because of his poor educational background, his inability to speak English, his lack of financial resources, and the discouraging comments by the people in Harare. He began to question whether attending the Bible College really was God's will for him. In the midst of his doubt and confusion, Peter fled to Nyanga where he had some friends from Mozambique. He was confused and unsure what to do. Once again God spoke to Peter, and told him that he needed to go back to Harare and attend the Bible College. With help from friends, Peter returned to Harare, and attended the Bible College.

Peter took three bibles to class: a Shona Bible (which was a dialect spoken in Zimbabwe), a Portuguese Bible (which he also spoke), and an English Bible. As a student Peter soon became discouraged and was faced with considerable doubt about his ability to complete the requirements for graduation. One of his biggest concerns was his inability to speak English, much less write and preach in English. Then, one morning when Peter awakened, he was not only able to understand English, he was able to speak and even write in English. This miracle reinforced his belief that God had special plans for him. Peter graduated from the Bible College in 1988 and began preaching in Zimbabwe. His ministry immediately began to bear fruit, and he was instrumental in establishing new churches.

Once again an angel appeared to Peter and instructed him to marry Lydia. At the wedding ceremony a man got up and proclaimed that Peter would go through a period of temptation, but he would emerge even stronger. Shortly after the wedding Lydia became pregnant. An angel appeared to Peter and told him he was going to have a son who should be called Stephen. The words of the angel came true, and Lydia delivered a baby boy whom they named Stephen. The temptation was in the form of Peter choosing to continue his successful ministry while God had other plans for him. Finally, Peter reluctantly agreed to leave that ministry and start an orphanage. In addition to the orphanage, Peter continued to preach and to establish more new churches.

Peter is the founder and head of African Ministries International. In this position he attempts to free people in Africa from their pagan practices and enable them to worship the Lord Jesus Christ. His vision in which Jesus said he was sending Peter to help others, and the vision in which God said He had plans for Peter, both turned out to be true.

How could a young boy who spent more than eight years living in the bush and in a concentration camp, blind in one eye, educated only through the fourth grade, enter the Bible College against the advice of everyone he knew, awaken one morning able to understand, speak and write English, graduate from the Bible College, and have a ministry that involved spreading the Gospel to thousands of people? Looking back over his life it is clear that God guided and protected Peter at every step in his journey. This didn't happen by accident or by coincidence. Peter's story is strong evidence that God exists and is active in the world today. Once again, undeniable prevails over inexplicable.

6

Threats to Christianity

Christianity in America is under attack like no other time in our history. Individuals and organizations such as the ACLU are challenging all forms of public Christian expression. Over the past few decades those challenges have multiplied, and their proponents have become much more aggressive. They argue that Christian activities such as Bible reading, prayer, and public displays of Christian symbols violate the principle of separation of church and state and the Establishment Clause which is part of the First Amendment to the Constitution.

Unfortunately, many people are unaware of the source of the phrase, separation of church and state, and its original intent. Many books have been written on this subject from a variety of perspectives.

> **Fact 1:** The phrase *separation of church and state* does not appear in any official founding document including the Constitution and the Declaration of Independence. It arose from a letter dated Jan. 1, 1802 from President Thomas Jefferson to the Danbury Baptist Association.

Comment: President Jefferson's letter was written in response to a letter dated October 7, 1801, which was sent to him by the Danbury Baptist Association of Danbury, Connecticut. The Danbury Baptists believed strongly that freedom of religion was a right given by God. They were concerned that the federal government might someday wrongly assert that it had the power to regulate public religious activities. The Danbury Baptists communicated their concern to President Jefferson. In response to their letter Jefferson stated:

> Believing with you that religion is a matter which lies solely between man and his God; that he owes account to none other for his faith or his worship; that the legislative powers of government reach actions only and not opinions; I contemplate with sovereign reverence that act of the whole American people which declared that their legislature should "make no law respecting an establishment of religion or prohibiting the free exercise thereof," thus building a *wall of separation between Church and State* (emphasis added).[1]

The last portion of this quote is the source of the phrase, separation of church and state.

> **Fact 2:** The Establishment Clause and the Free Exercise clause are part of the First Amendment to the Constitution.

Comment: The Constitution did not address the relationship between the federal government and religion. On September 26, 1789, the Congress of the United States proposed to the state legislatures that 12 amendments be added to the Constitution which specifically addressed restrictions placed on the federal government in a variety of areas. The first two proposed amendments were rejected. The remaining ten amendments were adopted and comprise the Bill of Rights.

The First Amendment states:

> Congress shall make no law respecting an establishment of religion or prohibiting the free exercise thereof; or abridging the freedom of speech, or the press; or the right of the people peaceably to assemble, and to petition the government for a redress of grievances.

The clause, "Congress shall make no law respecting an establishment of religion," is referred to as the Establishment Clause. The clause, "or

---

[1]   www.loc.gov/loc/clb/9806/danpre/html.

prohibiting the free exercise thereof," is referred to as the Free Exercise Clause.

> **Fact 3:** The original intent of the Establishment Clause and the Free Exercise Clause was to restrict the actions of the federal government. Neither clause was intended to restrict the religious expression of citizens.

Comment: In the discussions leading up to the final wording of these amendments as recorded in the Congressional Record, one dominant concern was the potential tyranny that could be imposed on citizens by the federal government. One of those concerns involved the establishment of a single denomination as the national religion similar to what the founders had witnessed in Great Britain and elsewhere. The First Amendment prohibits this action, and it also forbids the federal government from interfering with freedom of speech and the press. Very simply, the Founding Fathers did not want a federally mandated single denomination to rule America, but they did expect basic biblical principles and values to be an integral part of society.

> **Fact 4:** Virtually all of the Founding Fathers believed that religious faith was one of the most important virtues in a civil society. This faith guided the establishment of the new nation. The practice of religion was strongly encouraged by our Founding Fathers. Evidence of their faith is contained in many of their letters, policies and memoirs.

Comment: The history of the United States is closely aligned with Judeo-Christian values and beliefs. All of our leaders during the Revolution and the founding of our nation believed in a supreme being. Most were Christians.

> **Fact 5:** Thirty-seven states use the word God in the Preamble to their constitutions. Four other states— New Hampshire, Oregon, Tennessee and Virginia— use the word God elsewhere in their constitutions. The constitutions of the other nine states use other terms such as Supreme Ruler of the Universe, Divine

Goodness, Grateful for Divine Guidance, Author of Existence and Creator which acknowledge the existence of a supernatural being.

Comment: The founding documents do not require that a person must worship God or must practice a specific religion. However, those who desire to eliminate Christianity attempt to rewrite history by denying our Christian heritage. David Barton provides a detailed account of the religious background of the Founding Fathers. He summarizes his findings as follows:

> The evidence is clear that not only can none of them (Founding Fathers) be called an atheist, only the smallest handful would fit today's definition of a deist.[2]

Remark: A deist is a person who believes in the existence of a God who created the world, but who has not interacted with the world.

That Christianity played a very important role in our founding is evidenced not only by the writings of our Founding Fathers, but in actions of the Congress, some of which are listed below.

i.   The words "In God We Trust" appear on our currency.
ii. Each session of Congress opens with prayer.
iii. The Ten Commandments have been prominently displayed in many public buildings.
iv. National holidays such as Christmas were established by Congress.
v.   Weekly church services were held in the capitol building for nearly 100 years. These services were attended by numerous presidents and by many members of Congress.
vi. Bible study was strongly encouraged in public schools.
vii. At the beginning of each session of the Supreme Court the justices stand as the crier declares, "God save the United States and this honorable court."

---

[2]   David Barton, **Original Intent**, p. 149

For over 100 years these practices were unchallenged by any legal action.

The Christian heritage of the United States and its positive impact on the developing nation were clearly articulated by Alexis de Tocqueville in 1838 in his classic work, *The Republic of the States of America, and Its Political Institutions, Reviewed and Examined* (more commonly known as *Democracy in America*).

> Upon my arrival in the United States, the religious aspect of the country was the first thing that struck my attention; and the longer I stayed there, the more did I perceive the great political consequences resulting from this state of things, to which I was unaccustomed. In France I had almost always seen the spirit of religion and the spirit of freedom marching in pursuing courses diametrically opposed to each other; but in America, I found that they were intimately united and that they reigned in common over the same country.[3]

> The Americans combine the notions of Christianity and of liberty so intimately in their minds that it is impossible to make them conceive the one without the other.[4]

The Christian heritage of the United States was also recognized by Achille Murat in *A Moral and Political Sketch of the United States, 1833*. Murat, who strongly disliked religion, states:

> It must be admitted that looking at the physiognomy [discernible character] of the United States, its religion is the only feature which disgusts a foreigner....[T]here is no country in which the people are so religious as in the United States; to the eyes of a foreigner they even appear to be too much so.[5]

---

[3] quoted in David Barton, **Original Intent**, p. 127.
[4] quoted in David Barton, **Original Intent**, p. 291.
[5] quoted in David Barton, **Original Intent**, p. 127

Harriet Martineau, *Society in America, 1837*, who also had no love for religion, states:

> The institutions of America are, as I have said, planted down deep into Christianity. Its spirit must make an effectual pilgrimage through a society of which it may be called a native, and no mistrust of its influence can forever intercept that spirit in its mission of denouncing anomalies, exposing hypocrisy, rebuking faithlessness, raising and communing with the outcast, and driving out sordidness [vileness] from the circuit of this, the most glorious temple of society that has ever yet been reared.[6]

The view that the First Amendment was intended to prohibit the federal government from restricting religious expression by citizens is not shared by secular progressives. They insist that the First Amendment limits the public expression of Christianity. However, this interpretation is at odds with the interpretation and with the actions of the Founding Fathers and the Congress in the early days of our nation's history as described above. If their intent was to prohibit the public expression of Christianity, would they have encouraged prayer and bible reading in the public schools? Would the 10 Commandments be put on display in many public buildings? Would each session of Congress and each session of the Supreme Court be opened with a prayer? Would the words "In God we trust" appear on our currency? Would the constitutions of all 50 states contain references to a supernatural being?

In the application of a statute the legislative intent is of paramount importance. What were the writers of the statute trying to achieve? If the application of the law runs contrary to the legislative intent, then the statute is not being properly applied.

> When the intent undergirding a law is abandoned, then that law can be applied in a manner that is totally contrary to its intended purpose; the result can be devastating.[7]

---

[6] quoted in David Barton, **Original Intent**, p. 128
[7] David Barton, **Original Intent**. p. 153

Some enemies of Christianity argue that the Constitution is a living document that should be interpreted to fit contemporary conditions which take precedence over the original intent of the statute. We are witnessing a re-writing of history by those who deny our Christian heritage and who relentlessly attempt to remove Christianity from our culture and as the basis for our freedom and for our society. Some of their success is a result of the corruption of the legal system, the ignorance and naïveté of the public through lack of education, and media bias. The words of George Orwell in the novel *1984* describe their approach:

> Who controls the past controls the future. Who controls the present controls the past.

The question then becomes, how could a complete reversal of the original intent of the First Amendment possibly occur? The reversal did not happen overnight. The change in the interpretation of the phrase, *wall of separation*, from preventing the government from interfering with religion to preventing public expression of religious beliefs began in the mid-twentieth century.

McCollum v. Board of Education

In 1940, the Champaign (Illinois) Council on Religious Education, which consisted of Jewish, Roman Catholic, and some Protestant denominations, obtained permission from the Champaign Board of Education to offer classes in religious instruction for children in grades four through nine and for upper level grades. These classes were held during the school day. Instructors for the classes had to be approved by the superintendent. Attendance was voluntary and required written permission by parents. Students who did not attend these classes spent the time in other areas of the school.

In 1945 an atheist named Vashti McCollum filed suit against the Board of Education claiming that these classes violated the Establishment Clause of the First Amendment. In 1946 the Circuit Court of Champaign County ruled in the school district's favor. The case was appealed to the Illinois State Supreme Court which also ruled in the school district's favor. However, on March 8, 1948 the U. S. Supreme Court ruled 8–1 in favor of McCollum.

Engle v. Vitale

In 1951 the New York State Board of Regents approved the following nondenominational prayer for recital in the public schools.

> Almighty God, we acknowledge our dependence upon Thee, and we beg Thy blessings upon us, our parents, our teachers and our Country.

The Regents believed that the prayer would promote character development and good citizenship among the students. The Union Free School District No. 9 in New Hyde Park, New York, directed the principal to have the prayer recited aloud in the presence of a teacher in each class at the beginning of the school day. Students were not required to recite the prayer. Students who wished to be excused from the room while the prayer was being recited were given permission to go to another room.

The parents of ten students (Engel) objected to the prayer and filed suit in a New York State court in an effort to ban the prayer. They claimed that the prayer was contrary to their beliefs and the beliefs of their children. The state court ruled that the prayer did not violate the law as long as the school permitted the students to remain silent or to be excused from the room while the prayer was being recited. This ruling was appealed to the Supreme Court.

In 1962 the Supreme Court ruled in *Engel v. Vitale* that reciting the nondenominational prayer was unconstitutional. The Court stated that the First Amendment was not a limitation on the government, but a limitation on the public expression of religious faith by an individual. The majority opinion written by Justice Hugo Black states:

> We think that by using its public school system to encourage recitation of the Regents' Prayer, the State of New York has adopted a practice wholly inconsistent with the Establishment Clause.[8]

---

[8] www.infoplease.com/us/supreme-court/cases/ar10html#ixzz1niCdUMI

Murray v. Curlett and the School District of Abington Township v. Schempp

In 1905 the School Board of the Baltimore City Schools adopted a rule requiring public schools to open the school day by reading from the Bible and reciting the Lord's Prayer. In 1959 an atheist, Madalyn Murray, challenged the legality of these opening exercises. She filed suit against the school board claiming the exercises violated her constitutional rights and the rights of her son, William. A local judge dismissed the case. The case was appealed to the Court of Appeals in Maryland which also ruled that Bible reading and the recitation of the Lord's Prayer did not violate either the First or Fourteenth Amendments. The case was then appealed to the United States Supreme Court.

The same time this case was proceeding through the courts Edward Schempp filed suit against the Abington Township school district. Schempp claimed that the 1949 Pennsylvania state law which required that the school day should begin by reading without comment a minimum of ten verses from the Bible violated the First Amendment.

The District Court ruled in Schempp's favor. However, during the legal process the state amended the law so that students could be excused from the opening exercises upon receiving written permission from parent or guardian. Based upon the amended law, the Supreme Court remanded the case back to the District Court. The District Court again ruled in favor of Schempp and the case was appealed to the Supreme Court.

The Supreme Court consolidated the two cases, Murray v. Curlett and Abington Township v. Schempp. The question before the court was whether Bible reading and prayer in the public schools violated the First Amendment. The Supreme Court heard the case on February 27–28, 1963. On June 17, 1963, the court voted 8–1 that these actions were unconstitutional.

Remark: William Murray became a Christian in 1980. When his mother became aware of his conversion she proclaimed, "One could call this a postnatal abortion on the part of a mother, I guess. I repudiate him entirely and completely for now and all time … he is beyond human forgiveness." In his book, *My Life Without God*, Murray lamented that his mother: was blatantly evil, and she misused the trust of people and cheated children out of their parents' inheritance.

Since 1971 the Supreme Court has used a three-part test for deciding whether the principle of "Separation of Church and State" has been violated. A law or some action by a government agent or a school official will be declared unconstitutional under the test if it does not have a secular purpose, advances or inhibits religion, or fosters excessive government entanglement with religion.

There are hundreds of examples of how government agents at various levels and school officials have declared that Christian expression of almost any kind violates the principle of Separation of Church and State. Five examples of these rulings are given below.

Example 1: The 10 Commandments in Kentucky Classrooms

The state of Kentucky passed a law requiring that a copy of the Ten Commandments be posted in each public school classroom. Sydell Stone and a number of other parents filed suit against the superintendent of public schools in Kentucky challenging this law.

The question before the court was whether the Kentucky statute violated the Establishment Clause of the First Amendment. In 1980, in a 5–4 per curiam decision, (a ruling by an appellate court consisting of multiple judges in which the decision is made by a majority of the jurists acting collectively and anonymously) the court ruled that the Kentucky law violated the Establishment Clause of the Constitution. The Court found the requirement that the Ten Commandments be posted "had no secular legislative purpose" and was "plainly religious in nature." The Court noted that the Ten Commandments did not confine themselves to arguably secular matters (such as murder, stealing, etc.), but rather concerned matters such as the worship of God and the observance of the Sabbath.

Example 2: Berkeley Gardens Elementary School in Denver, Colorado

In 1987 two parents complained to Kathleen Madigan, the principal at the Berkeley Gardens Elementary School, that a fifth grade teacher, Kenneth Roberts, had two books, *The Bible in Pictures* and *The Story of Jesus*, in his 240-book classroom library. Principal Madigan ordered the books removed. She explained that the principle of Separation of Church and State made such action necessary. Principal Madigan also noticed that Roberts kept a Bible on his desk along with other books. She told him to keep it out of sight during classroom hours. On another occasion, Madigan told Roberts not to read silently from his Bible while his students read silently from books of their choice.

When Roberts pressed for some written guidelines, Madigan reaffirmed her earlier instructions, stating, "The law is clear that religion may not be taught in school. To avoid the appearance of teaching religion, I have given you this directive." Roberts sued Madigan and the Adams County School District No. 50, seeking monetary damages and a declaration that they had acted unlawfully. The justices, without comment, let stand rulings that the orders from the school principal were valid and did not amount to unlawful hostility toward Christianity.

Example 3: Prayer at the Santa Fe Independent School District in Texas

In April, 1995, two unidentified students in the Santa Fe Independent School District filed suit in the Federal District Court objecting to student prayers over the public address system prior to home football games. The students (referred to as the Does in the suit) claimed that the prayers violated the Establishment Clause of the Constitution. During the litigation process the school district made some changes in their policy. One change was that an election would take place to determine whether students wanted to continue offering invocations prior to football games. The students voted in favor of continuing the prayers. A second change was that elections would be held to determine which student would offer the prayer.

In 1996 the District Court ruled in favor of the school district based on these revisions, provided that the prayers were nonsectarian and non-proselytizing. Both the school district and the Does appealed this ruling. The school district objected to the portion of the ruling which dictated that the prayers must be nonsectarian and non-proselytizing. The Does claimed that the prayers were unconstitutional.

In June, 2000, the Court of Appeals ruled that despite the modifications described above, allowing prayer at football games violated the Establishment Clause. The verdict was appealed. The Supreme Court also ruled that permitting prayer initiated by students and led by students violated the Establishment Clause.

Example 4: Santa Rosa County School District in Florida

In 2009 the ACLU sued the Santa Rosa County School District on behalf of two students who complained that some teachers and administrators allowed prayer at school events such as graduation ceremonies. The school district settled out of court with the ACLU. As part of the settlement agreement the school district barred all school employees from promoting prayer at school sponsored events. The agreement also barred the school district from holding events at church venues when a secular alternative was available. In addition, the district agreed to prevent the senior class president from speaking at the commencement ceremonies because, as a Christian, she might say something religious. (Source: Washington Times website)

Example 5: The ACLU and the Pittsylvania County Board of Supervisors in Virginia

In 2011 the ACLU of Virginia sued the Pittsylvania County Board of Supervisors in an attempt to prevent them from opening their meetings with prayer, which the ACLU claimed violated the First Amendment. Kent Willis, the ACLU Executive Director in Virginia stated:

> The government should never use its power to promote one religion over others. That is why the first clause of

the First Amendment prohibits the government from establishing religion, and why the courts have made it clear that formal prayers at legislative meetings must be broad and inclusive rather than focusing on a particular religion."

Tim Barber, Chairman of the Board of Supervisors, responded that the board would continue its regular practice of prayers before meetings, and that he would be willing to go to court over the issue. Barber also stated that the Board of Supervisors was standing up for what is right and that it is time for the American public to oppose groups like the ACLU that want to tear down the very foundations on which this great country was built.

The following statements summarize the rulings in these cases:

1. Religious instruction during the school day is unconstitutional despite the fact that students must receive permission by their parents to attend these classes. That students not attending religious classes spent this class time in other rooms was not relevant.
2. Reciting a nondenominational prayer in the presence of a teacher in a public school is unconstitutional despite the fact that students are not required to recite the prayer and may choose to go to another room where the prayer is not being recited during this time period.
3. Posting the Ten Commandments in a public school classroom violates the Establishment Clause of the Constitution and is, therefore, illegal.
4. A teacher may not have a Christian book in his/her classroom library and may not have the Bible on his/her desk while students are present because "religion should not be taught in school".
5. Allowing student-led prayer over a public address system prior to a football game violates the Establishment Clause.
6. The ACLU states on their website that "public schools themselves should not be in the business

of promoting particular religious beliefs or religious activities. ... public schools should not be leading children in prayers or religious ceremonies..." They have argued that allowing prayer at school events such as commencement ceremonies violates the Establishment Clause, and therefore, is illegal. As part of the out of court settlement school employees were barred from promoting prayer at school sponsored events, and the school district prohibited the senior class president from speaking at commencement ceremonies because she might say something religious.

7. The ACLU sued the County Board of Supervisors to prevent them from opening their meetings with prayer.

In contrast to the actions against Christian activities, consider the case involving the Union School District in Byron, California.

The ACLU and the Union School District in Byron California

The California State Board of Education requires that 7th grade world history classes contain a unit on Islamic history, culture, and religion. The state approved the textbook, *Across the Centuries*, for use in these classes. This textbook was used at the Excelsior School in the Byron Union School district during a three week study of Islam during the fall semester in 2001. Excelsior teachers were also encouraged to use other instructional methods. Some teachers chose to use an interactive educational module called, "Islam: A simulation of Islamic history and culture". The module encouraged role-play activities to simulate the five pillars of faith in the Muslim religion. In one class the teacher distributed a Student Guide which states that "from the beginning [of this module] you and your classmates will become Muslims."

During this three-week period the following activities were part of the study.

Students were required to study the five pillars of Islam which are essential to Sunni Islam.

The first two pillars of Islam are as follows:

i. Recite the **shahadah**: "I testify that there is none worthy of worship except God, and I testify that Muhammad is the Messenger of God". Most Muslims repeat this many times each day.
ii. Perform the **salat** which is a ritual prayer to be recited 5 times a day, if possible, with one's body pointed toward Mecca.

In discussing these pillars the teacher read Muslim prayers and portions of the Qur'an aloud in class. The teacher also required students to recite phrases from a Muslim prayer including, "In the name of God, Most Gracious, Most Merciful." Students were also required to make banners, some of which used words from the Qur'an which were also translated into English.

The third and fourth pillars of Islam are as follows:

iii. **Zakat**, the practice of giving alms to the poor and needy.
iv. **Sawmi,** the practice of fasting during the month of Ramadan.

In discussing the third and fourth pillars of Islam the teacher required students to perform volunteer community service projects and to give up activities such as watching television or eating certain foods to conform to Muslim practices for Ramadan.

The fifth pillar of Islam is **Hajj**:

If economically and physically possible, one must make at least one pilgrimage to Mecca during his or her lifetime. To demonstrate **Hajj** students were divided into teams and played a board game with the goal of arriving at Mecca.

One method used to present religious information involved the use of flash cards which were classified as fact or trivia. Cards that were declared to be factual included:

    i.   The Qur'an was God's third revelation to the Prophet Muhammad;

    ii. The Holy Qur'an is God's word.

These statements were presented as absolute truth with no qualifiers indicating that they were simply what Muslims believed to be true. The teacher encouraged, but did not require, students dress in Arab-style clothing.

As part of the final exam the teacher required students to critique Islamic culture based on their exposure to that culture and religion during this study. The assignment also included the warning: Be careful, if you do not have something positive to say, don't say anything.

The school district stated that students were given the option to be excused from this study, but parents claim they were not informed of this right. The study portrayed Islam very favorably. No mention was made of the history of Islam which is replete with terrorist attacks and with violence against nonbelievers in pursuit of world denomination by radical extremists. No mention was made of certain aspects of Islamic culture in many Muslim countries that are diametrically opposed to Western cultural values. For example, in some Muslim countries, a man may have up to four wives, but a woman can have only one husband. Women do not have the same rights as men. Women are not allowed to drive. There are very strict laws concerning how women must dress in public.

Jonas and Tiffany Eklund and their children sued the Byron School District charging that these teachings violated the Establishment Clause of the First Amendment. A hearing was held at the United States District Court, Northern District of California on December 3, 2003. A decision was rendered two days later in which district judge Phyllis Hamilton ruled that these activities did not violate the First Amendment. This verdict was appealed to the 9ᵗʰ Circuit Court of Appeals. In 2005 a three judge panel also ruled that there was no conflict with the principle of Separation of Church and State with this study of Islamic culture and religion. In 2006 the Supreme Court declined to hear the case.

Remark: The 9ᵗʰ Circuit Court of Appeals is the same court that ruled that a cross on public property in the middle of the desert violates the Constitution.

When it comes to the religion of Islam, the following actions evidently do not violate the principle of Separation of Church and State.

1. Religious classes may be held during the school day on school property even if students are not permitted to be excused from those classes.
2. A teacher reading aloud from the Qur'an, leading students in the recitation of Muslim prayers, and requiring students to memorize and recite verses from the Qur'an does not violate the First Amendment, in contrast to reading verses from the Bible and reciting the Lord's Prayer to begin the school day, or reciting a prayer before a football game or at a school event such as commencement.
3. Displaying posters prepared by students containing quotations from the Qur'an which have been translated into English does not violate the Establishment Clause while simply posting the Ten Commandments in the classroom does.
4. Requiring students to observe the five pillars of Islam during this study, having them recite the claim that the Qur'an is the word of God, that Muhammad is the Messenger of God, and that these statements are true do not violate the Supreme Court directive that an action cannot advance a religion.

There was no attempt by the ACLU or any other organization active in the effort to eliminate Christianity in the public square to oppose these actions. Their approach, the ruling of the 9th Circuit Court of Appeals, and the decision of the U. S. Supreme Court not to hear this case are all undeniably hypocritical.

Tactics used by the enemies of Christianity

In *Rules for Radicals* (1971) Saul Alinsky provides a detailed and effective manual for those who desire to change society and who are willing to use any means to accomplish their ends. His eleven rules are:

1. Concern about ethics, means and ends varies inversely with one's personal interest in the issue.
2. Judgment of the ethics is dependent upon the political position of those sitting in judgment.
3. In war the end justifies almost any means.

Comment: Alinsky argues that honesty, integrity, and truth need not be considered in making an argument in support of one's cause. The truth can, and in many cases, should be distorted or completely disregarded.

4. Judgment must be made in the context of the times in which the action occurred and not from any other chronological vantage point.

Comment: According to Alinsky the Constitution is a living document that can be interpreted independent of its original intent if such an interpretation supports the cause.

5. The concern with ethics increases with the number of means available, and vice versa.
6. The less important the end to be desired, the more one can afford to engage in ethical evaluations of means.
7. Generally, success or failure is a mighty determinant of ethics. (There can be no such thing as a successful traitor, for if one succeeds, he becomes a founding father.)

8. The morality of a means depends upon whether the means is being employed at a time of imminent defeat or imminent victory. (The same means with victory seemingly assured may be defined as immoral, whereas if it had been used in desperate circumstances to avert defeat, the question of morality would never arise.)

Comment: Alinsky contends that ethics and morality can be ignored if the point one is trying to make is important. They can be totally ignored in support of an argument if that argument is necessary to avoid defeat.

9. Any effective means is automatically judged by the opposition as being unethical.
10. Do what you can with what you have and clothe it with moral garments.
11. Goals must be phrased in general terms like liberty, equality, fairness, for the common welfare, pursuit of happiness, or bread and peace.

Comment: Alinsky maintains that if your argument is effective, you may be accused of being unethical. At the same time, if an argument used by an opponent is true and effective, attack the ethics, intelligence, and morality of the individual. Arguments should be expressed in terms of equality, the common good, and the necessity of eliminating favoritism of a certain group.

Some of the tactics used by secular progressives are clearly consistent with the tactics advocated by Saul Alinsky.

If America is indeed abandoning its Christian heritage, then the question must be asked, is God speaking to America? And if so, what is God saying, and how is America responding?

7

Is God Speaking to America?

How do you know when God is speaking to you? Believers and even non-believers have been asking this question for centuries. Many times the answer is simply, "Well, I just know it!" In reality, there is no answer that works for everyone. This chapter is focused on the question posed by Rabbi Jonathan Cahn in *The Harbinger* and the associated video, *Isaiah 9:10*:

Is God speaking to America, and if so, is America listening?

The Bible states that God spoke to ancient Israel. Many times God warned the people of Israel and their leaders to repent or face serious consequences. Is there is a relationship between ancient Israel and contemporary America? Are there similarities between the way Israel behaved and the way America is behaving? If their behaviors are similar, then, is it possible that God is speaking to America in the same way that God spoke to Israel? To help answer these questions consider some of the ways God spoke to Israel, and how Israel responded to God.

Ancient Israel

God chose Israel to fulfill a special mission:

> The Lord said to Abram, "Leave your country, your people and your father's household and go to the land I will show you. I will make you into a great nation, and I will bless you; I will make your name great, and you will be a blessing. I will bless those who bless you, and

whoever curses you I will curse; and all peoples of the
earth will be blessed through you," (Genesis 12: 1–3).

Abram and his descendants endured many hardships and suffered
through some very difficult times. After Moses led the Israelites out of
bondage in Egypt and into the Sinai Desert, God gave Moses the Ten
Commandments and a series of laws that the Israelites were to obey to
help mold the nation. While the Israelites were in the desert, God made
a covenant with the emerging nation.

> Now if you obey me fully and keep my covenant, then
> out of all nations you will be my treasured possession.
> Although the whole earth is mine you will be a kingdom
> of priests and a holy nation (Exodus 19:5-6).

This covenant was different from the covenant that God made with
Abram because God's continued blessing and shield of protection were
dependent upon their obedience to the laws that God gave to Moses.

After spending forty years in the desert, the Israelites began their
conquest of the Promised Land. Many years later under the leadership
of King David the Israelites completed their conquest. Israel prospered
under David and his son, Solomon, and became a major power in the
region. However, shortly after Solomon's death the nation was divided
into two kingdoms in 922 BC. The Northern Kingdom, Israel, and the
Southern Kingdom, Judah, periodically battled each other. As time
passed, Israel drifted away from its spiritual foundation and disobeyed
God. Their downward spiral culminated in idol worship, which included
child sacrifice, in an attempt to please pagan gods. Thus, Israel rejected
its covenant relationship with God.

Elijah, Elisha, Hosea, and Amos were prophets who challenged Israel to
repent. They warned that if Israel failed to repent, then Israel faced the
loss of God's blessings and the shield of protection from their enemies.

In 732 BC Israel was attacked by Assyria. The result was devastating, but
it could have been much worse. Assyria withdrew many of its forces, and
Israel gained a brief respite.

Israel's response to the invasion was captured by the prophet Isaiah.

> The bricks have fallen down, but we will rebuild with
> dressed stone; the sycamores trees have been cut down,
> but we will plant cedars in their place, (Isaiah 9:10).

The Israelites did not repent. Instead, they vowed to rebuild and become even stronger.

The context of Isaiah 9:10 makes it clear that the attack by Assyria was a warning by God that if the Israelites failed to repent, they would face future destruction. Israel's response to rebuild and become stronger was misguided and arrogant.

A decade later Assyria again attacked Israel. This time Assyria conquered Israel and many Israelites were exiled to other parts of the Middle East. Because the Israelites failed to repent, the fate they sought to avoid occurred. Their rebuilding effort and their attempt to become stronger were in vain.

Modern America

The Bible does not teach that America is God's chosen people. However, America has had a special mission to spread the gospel of Jesus Christ and to assist other nations in gaining their freedom. God has richly blessed America, and America has acknowledged its relationship with God from its very beginning.

President George Washington was inaugurated on April 30, 1789, which marked the birth of the new nation. The inauguration took place in New York City which was the nation's capital at the time. In his inaugural address, President Washington warned:

> We ought to be no less persuaded that the propitious
> smiles of Heaven can never be expected on a nation that
> disregards the eternal rules of order and right which
> Heaven itself has ordained.

Thus, George Washington warned that if America turned its back on God, then God would no longer bless America and would no longer protect America from its enemies.

After his inaugural address, President Washington, members of the cabinet, and members of Congress proceeded to St. Paul's Chapel to pray for God's providence and protection for the new nation. This act was an unmistakable message that America was launched with a strong Christian foundation.

Remark: St. Paul's Chapel still stands today. It is located at the edge of Ground Zero. On 9/11, the Chapel was spared from extensive damage and possible destruction by a sycamore tree. The tree, located next to the Chapel, was destroyed by debris when the second tower collapsed, but the Chapel survived with minimal damage.

For the first 150 years of America's existence, American culture strongly reflected its Christian heritage. This fact was validated by acts of Congress and the writings of Alexis de Tocqueville, Achille Murat, and Harriet Martineau in the 19th century as noted in chapter 6. God looked on America with great favor. The United States overcame many obstacles and experienced unprecedented prosperity. Today, America is the world's only superpower.

If de Tocqueville, Murat, and Martineau returned to America in the 21st century, would they reach the same conclusions they reached in the 19th century? Most would agree that their conclusions would be considerably different.

As noted in chapter 6, in the 20th century American culture began to drift away from its spiritual foundation. Over the past half-century Americans have shown increased apathy toward Christianity. Church attendance has declined. Biblical truth has been distorted in some venues to curry favor. Prayer and Bible reading have been prohibited in public schools. The Ten Commandments have been removed from public buildings. Courts have ruled that Christian activities including praying and displaying Christian symbols in the public square are unconstitutional. Personal responsibility and accountability often have been ignored and completely abandoned.

Immorality has been widely condoned and has invaded all areas of public life. This downward spiral has accelerated over the past few decades, and America's Christian heritage has become increasingly rejected.

Many Christian leaders have deplored these changes, but their words have largely fallen on deaf ears. America has been steadily abandoning its Christian roots and is becoming increasingly secular. Thus, both ancient Israel and contemporary America strayed from their religious foundation.

President Washington's warning came true on September 11, 2001 when a group of terrorists breached America's security and destroyed the World Trade Center, a symbol of America's economic might. They also destroyed a portion of the Pentagon, a symbol of America's military strength. As devastating as this attack proved to be, thus far there have been no follow-up attacks, and America has enjoyed a respite.

America's response to this attack was similar to Israel's response to the Assyrian invasion. On September 12, 2001, long before the dust settled at Ground Zero, Senate Majority Leader Tom Daschle spoke to the American people on behalf of Congress in response to the terrorist attack. Daschle quoted Isaiah 9:10 saying:

> The bricks have fallen down, but we will rebuild with dressed stone; the fig trees have been cut down, but we will replace them with cedars.

Daschle's intention was to encourage America to rebuild and become stronger. Apparently he was unaware of the fact that these words were part of God's warning to Israel. Thus, Daschle, unknowingly, was giving the same warning to America that Isaiah gave to Israel—repent or face destruction.

Immediately after 9/11 many religious leaders exhorted Americans to repent and restore the nation's Christian foundation. The response was short-lived, and all too soon America continued its sinful decline.

Question: Was the 9/11 attack a warning by God to repent and return to its Christian foundation or face future destruction?

Rabbi Jonathan Cahn cites nine harbingers that God gave Israel and identifies stunning parallels between them and the terrorist attacks on 9/11. After reading *The Harbinger* and watching *Isaiah 9:10*, most people would conclude that these parallels are not coincidental.

Cahn contends that just as the Assyrian attack on Israel in 732 BC was God's warning to Israel, the 9/11 attack was God's warning to America to repent or face future destruction. The above question can be restated as Proposition 5, and the consequences of its two possible truth values can be examined.

Proposition 5: The terrorist attack of 9/11 was a warning by God for America to repent and return to its Christian foundation or America will face future destruction.

If Proposition 5 is false, then the 9/11 attack was not a warning by God of future attacks and future destruction. If America rebuilds its defenses and solves its financial problems, it may well survive future attacks and possible economic meltdowns.

If Proposition 5 is true, then, if America repents and reclaims its Christian heritage, God will continue to bless America, and God will protect America from its enemies. However, if America does not repent, it will make no difference if America rebuilds its defenses in an attempt to become stronger because America will face consequences far more devastating than the attack on 9/11.

The Harbinger is written as a novel, and the main character was asked:

> What if it were you who heard the voice of the prophets, and understood the Harbingers, and knew the judgment was coming? Everyone around you was oblivious to it. Everyone just went on with their lives with no idea of what was coming. What would you do?[1]

In answer to that question, America's leaders and the American people must ask God for guidance on how to lead the nation back to its Christian

---

[1] Jonathan Cahn, *The Harbinger* (2011), p. 226-227

foundation. Americans must repent, and pray for forgiveness. America needs to be reminded of II Chronicles 7:14.

> If my people, who are called by my name, will humble themselves and pray and seek my face and turn from their wicked ways, then I will hear from heaven and will forgive their sin and will heal their land.

If the harbingers are true, and if America fails to repent and return to its Christian roots, what does this mean for America's future and for our children and our grandchildren?

In the 21st century America is facing a financial crisis due to high unemployment, widespread corruption at all levels of government, exploding national debt and massive unfunded liabilities that will wreak havoc on the American way of life. It is possible that America will be faced with increased social unrest similar to what has been happening in Europe. Significant cuts in national security coupled with rogue nations developing weapons of mass destruction are making America increasingly vulnerable to a national catastrophe. America is in desperate need of God's protective shield.

8

Conclusions

The following two questions were asked at the beginning of chapter 1:

1. Does God exist?
2. What is the origin of life on earth, and in particular, human life?

The first question was transformed into Proposition 1:

Proposition 1: An Infinite Intelligent Entity (IIE) exists.

If Proposition 1 is true, then the second question was transformed into Proposition 2:

Proposition 2: The Infinite Intelligent Entity (IIE) created life on earth, including human life.

If both Proposition 1 and Proposition 2 are true, then this led to a third proposition.

Proposition 3: There is life after death.

If any of the above propositions is false, then the consequences are similar. They lead to a dead end. However, if all three propositions are true, then this led to a fourth proposition:

Proposition 4: Jesus, the Son of God, as described in the New Testament, was a living being who came to earth about 2,000 years ago.

The propositions and their consequences were summarized in the following diagram.

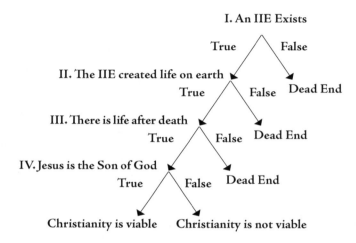

Accepting or rejecting Jesus Christ as Lord and Savior is not just about where we spend eternity. This decision also has a profound effect on our life on earth. Accepting Jesus does not mean that we will avoid pain and suffering or dealing with difficult circumstances. We are sinners. We live in an imperfect world. God will give us the strength we need to endure difficult times. We can live with an inner peace that is not possible without God. The bottom line is: either Jesus is the Lord of all, or not lord at all.

Imagine the following scenario. You are home alone. Suddenly, you feel a searing pain in your chest. Your breathing is labored. You feel lightheaded and are concerned about passing out. You lie down. You believe you are having a heart attack.

You consider two options in response to your life-threatening situation. One is to do nothing and simply accept your fate knowing that your life will probably be over very soon. The second option is to grab your cell phone and dial 911 in an attempt to save your life. For most people the decision is easy – make the phone call and choose life.

Next, consider the similarity in options available in the scenario described above to the options available in the following scenario.

Sooner or later each of us must die. Death may occur in the near future or perhaps many years down the road. Recognizing that someday you will die leaves you with two options. You can deny God's existence, believe that there is no life after death, and accept the consequences if you are wrong—which would involve spending eternity in an existence far worse than you could ever imagine.

The second option, which is analogous to the lifesaving 911 call, is to get down on your knees and pray. The prayer is simple. Tell God that you believe that Jesus Christ is His Son, and that you accept Jesus as Lord and Savior.

Which option you choose is up to you. It cannot be avoided. God does not force Himself on you. Accepting Jesus Christ as your personal savior has implications far beyond where you spend eternity. It provides you with an opportunity to experience a far more meaningful life on earth. You can experience a peace that goes far beyond anything the world has to offer. Reading the Bible and worshipping with other believers gives one a new purpose for life on earth. If you haven't had this experience, you have no idea what you are missing. The choice is simple: choose life and choose it today.

Bibliography

1. Alinsky, Saul D., *Rules for Radicals*, Vintage Books, New York, 1971.

2. Behe, Michael, *Darwin's Black Box*, The Free Press, New York, 1996.

3. *The Edge of Evolution*, The Free Press, New York, 2007.

4. Behe, Michael, Dembski, William, Meyer, Stephen, "Science and Evidence for Design in the Universe", Papers Presented at a conference sponsored by the Wethersfield Institute, New York, September 1999.

5. Cahn, Jonathan, *The Harbinger*, Frontline, Lake Mary, FL, 2011.

6. Corso, Col Philip (Ret.) with William J. Birnes, *The Day After Rosewell*, New York: Pocket Books, 1997.

7. Coyne, Jerry A., *Why Evolution is True*, Viking, New York, 2009.

8. Dawkins, Richard, *The Selfish Gene*, Oxford University Press, New York, 1989.

9. *Climbing Mount Improbable*, Oxford University Press, New York, 1996.

10. *The Blind Watchmaker*, Oxford University Press, New York, 1996.

11. *The Ancestor's Tale*, Houghton Mifflin Company, New York, 2004

12. Dawkins, Richard, *The God Delusion*, First Mariner Books Edition, New York, NY, 2006.

13. Dembski, William, *Intelligent Design*, InterVarsity Press, Downers Grove, IL, 1999.

14. Dembski, William and Kushiner, James. *Signs of Intelligence*, Brazos Press, Grand Rapids, MI, 2001.

15. Dennett, Daniel C., *Darwin's Dangerous Idea*, Simon & Schuster Paperbacks, New York, 1995.

16. DeYoung, Don, *Thousands ... Not Billions*, Master Books, Inc., Green Forest, AZ, 2005.

17. D'Souza, Dinesh, *What's So Great About Christianity*, Regency Publishing, Inc., Washington DC, 2004.

18. Gallups, Carl, *The Magic Man in the Sky*, WND Books, 2012.

19. Gonzalez, Guillermo and Richards, Jay W., *The Privileged Planet: How Our Place in the Cosmos is Designed for Discovery*, Regnery Publishing Company, Washington, DC, 2004.

20. Harris, Sam, *Letter to a Christian Nation*, Alfred A. Knopf, New York, 2007.

21. Hitchens, Christopher, *god is not Great*, 237 Park Ave., Hatchette Book Group USA, New York, 2007.

22. Johnson, Phillip E., *Darwin on Trial*, InterVarsity Press, Downers Grove, IL, 1993.

23. Perloff, James, *The Case Against Darwin*, Refuge Books, Burlington, MA, 2002.

24. Perloff, James, *Tornado in a Junkyard*, Refuge Books, Burlington, MA, 1999.

25. Rosen, Kenneth H., *Discrete Mathematics and Its Applications*, Vol. 4, McGraw-Hill, Boston, 1999.

26. Ross, Hugh, *The Creator and the Cosmos*, Navpress, Colorado Springs, 1993.

27. Sarfati, Jonathan, *Refuting Revolution*, Master Books, Green Forest, AZ, 1999.

28. Sarfati, Jonathan, *Refuting Revolution 2*, Master Books, Green Forest, AZ, 2002.

29. Stenger, Victor, *God, The Failed Hypothesis*, Prometheus Books, Amherst, NY, 2007.

30. Strobel, Lee, *The Case for Christ*, Zondervan Publishing House, Grand Rapids, MI, 1998.

31. Ward, Peter D. and Brownlee, Donald, *Rare Earth*, Copernicus, New York, NY, 2000.

32. Wells, Jonathan, *Icons of Evolution*, Regnery Publishing, Washington, DC, 2002.

Printed in the United States
By Bookmasters